INVITATION TO
AWAKEN

INVITATION TO AWAKEN

Embracing Our Natural
State of Presence

TONY PARSONS

InnerDirections
PUBLISHING

InnerDirections Publishing

INNER DIRECTIONS®
P.O. Box 130070
Carlsbad, California 92013
Tel: 800 545-9118 • 760 599-4075
www.InnerDirections.org

Cover and interior design by Joan Greenblatt

Printed in Canada on recycled paper

ISBN: 1-878019-21-X

Library of Congress Catalog Card Number: 2003115499

This book is

dedicated to Claire.

Love beyond the

speaking of it.

In Gratitude

To all of those who have helped in their own particular way to spread this message:

Rose Youd, Michael Angress, Chris Harwood, John Ryan, Ricky James, Julian & Catherine Noyce, Brian Holden, Haydn Davies, Terry Sullivan, Janet Marsh, Roger Hart, Habiba, Annie Wilson, Evor Hines, Roger Linden, Michael Reid, Nathan Gill, Jan Kersschot, Leo Hartong, Philip & Denise Boerma, Belle Bruins, Aidan & Kathleen Harrison, Wouter Schopman, Angela Renner & Kees Melse, Hetty de Vries, Janna Schagen, Philippe de Henning, Marianne Nentwig, Margit & Laszlo Jacob, Dan Feldman, Linda Hubly, Carol & Mark O'Laughlin, Ronald S. Miller, Phyllis Kahaney, Matthew & Joan Greenblatt of Inner Directions, and our other publishers in Holland, Germany, Spain, and France; and to everyone else who has participated in this wonderful adventure.

Table
of
Contents

All there is is this . . . and that . . .
    being
        the one appearing as two
        nothing appearing as everything
        the absolute appearing as the particular
        emptiness appearing as fullness
        the uncaused appearing as the caused
        unicity appearing as separation
        subject appearing as object
        the singular appearing as plurality
        the impersonal appearing as the personal
        the unknown appearing as the known.

    It is silence sounding and stillness moving
    and these words appearing as pointers
    to the wordless
        . . . and yet nothing is happening.

Preface

"When the apparent separate
identity falls away, the radiant
wonder of presence becomes
apparent to no one."

I am surprised at the number of teachings that are presented
or thought of as nondualistic or Advaita teachings when
they are anything but. As far as I can see, the radical, clear,
and uncompromising expression of absolute nondualism is still
very rarely communicated. There are plenty of "well-known"
teachers or masters who seem to subscribe to the concept of
Advaita yet constantly contradict its real meaning with their
teachings and recommendations.

It seems that this kind of confused communication is

generated either from a lack of real clarity or from personal motivation. The reality is that the two perspectives do not meet in any way. So where is the fundamental difference?

The word Advaita means "not two" and expresses as nearly as possible in words the perception that all and everything is already oneness or unicity, and that there is nothing else but "that." When this is clearly seen, it completely exposes the idea of subject and object merely as an illusory concept held within the hypnotic dream of separation. Consequently, the idea that an apparently separate individual (subject) can choose to attain something called enlightenment (object) becomes completely irrelevant. It also becomes clear that all practices or effort to follow a path leading to a future goal continuously reinforces the sense of the seeker and the sought, which is a direct denial of abiding unicity.

The argument that presumes that dualistic practices can lead the apparent seeker to the nondualistic perception is similar to the idea that with sufficient effort and determination, you can teach a blind man to see. This point is addressed in *As It Is: The Open Secret of Spiritual Awakening*:

> Doctrines, processes and progressive paths which seek enlightenment only exacerbate the problem they address by reinforcing the idea that the self can find something it presumes it has lost. It is that very effort, that investment in self-identity, that continuously recreates the illusion of separation from oneness. This is the veil that we believe exists. It is the dream of individuality.

The many awakenings that have recently been described to me continuously confirm that one of the first realizations to arise is the seeing that there is no one and nothing to awaken.

And yet, we see that the majority of so-called Advaita teachers, some of whom are revered, have been and still are constantly speaking to an apparent separate seeker (subject). They recommend that in order to attain enlightenment (object), one should choose to meditate, self-inquire, purify, cultivate understanding, still the mind and the ego, surrender, be honest, seek earnestly, give up seeking, do therapy, do nothing, be here now, and so on. The ideas are as endless and as complicated as the minds from where they are generated.

The basic ignorance concerning the teaching of becoming is generated by the teacher who believes that he or she has personally attained enlightenment through choice and effort, and that their disciples can do the same. But "who" is it that is going to choose to make the effort? How can an illusion dispel itself?

The concept of personal enlightenment arises within the mind, which sets up a false structure consisting of a "spiritual ego" or so-called "higher self," which has adapted or is attracted to a whole set of taught ideals concerning the need for self-purification, which it believes will eventually bring about the prize of enlightenment. It then attempts to discipline the so-called "lower self" to carry out tasks which appear to be contrary to its nature. This is the source of all of the struggle, confusion, sense of inadequacy, and disillusionment that abounds in the search. It is also the main reason that, until recently, enlightenment has seemed to be a rare occurrence. Of course, all of this confusion is as much an expression of oneness as clarity is.

In reality, what is longed for is absence—the absence of the "me" that seeks and feels separate. From this absence emerges the wonder and delight of what is. This is pure Advaita, which is not a teaching and is beyond understanding and the mind's limited ideas of becoming, destiny, karma, and personal attainment.

However, within the apparent drama of the search for oneness, we are witnessing a new readiness to really hear this rare but uncompromisingly clear message of absolute nondualism. Already the effect is profoundly liberating.

When the illusory separate identity falls away, the radiant wonder of presence becomes apparent to no one. It also becomes clear that there was no one who ever needed to be liberated. This theme runs continuously through *Invitation to Awaken*. If you dip into it rather than plod through it page by page, looking for "the answer," you could begin to sense a flavor of something that is beyond answers.

Throughout this book, discussions take place on several levels. The first is the exchange of concepts, within which context confused ideas about our original nature can be displaced by a clarity that is both uncompromising and mysterious. At another level, what is being shared in silence is already known. Wisdom speaks to wisdom, nothing speaks to nothing, and it is recognized that we meet and resonate with that which already is.

The message of this book is a totally radical and uncompromising expression of absolute nondualism. It bypasses the mind and speaks to the very core of a wisdom that is inherent in all of us. When there is a readiness to hear, all seeking and need for personal endeavor falls away, leaving the simple wonder of what is.

Tony Parsons
Cornwall, England

CHAPTER ONE

La Jolla

Inner Directions Gathering

"You are the divine
expression; everything is the
divine expression."

I walked away from religion. As far as I was concerned, the Christian religion helped hide the secret. Although it *appeared* to hold the secret, it was actually hidden. In a book called *The Mark*, Maurice Nicoll interprets the word "repent." I always thought it meant to be sorry for your sins and never to sin again. Actually, as far as Nicoll was concerned, it means "to turn around 180 degrees and see everything anew." In some way, the sentence in that book opened everything for me and started my inquiry.

I began to understand what healing the blind means in the Gospels, and I asked, very deeply, not just intellectually, but with every fiber of my being, to have my eyes opened. I was ready to give up everything for just one glimpse of that mystery. Three days later, while walking across the park, I was no longer doing the walking. There was simply the *presence* of walking, and in that indescribable state, stillness and overwhelming love permeated everything.

Along with the experience of the "indescribable" came a great clarity about it. After living in that space for quite some time, I began to stop "understanding" it and just lived it. I think there has to be a period where this perception is embraced and embodied, and this obviously took me some time. Later on, I also embraced and realized the nondualistic view that there is "no one," and therefore nothing can be done to achieve "this." We cannot move toward "this" since there is no one to do the moving. There is no one: this is it! Although my first book, *The Open Secret*, was written in 1995, only later did speaking to people in a more public way begin to take place.

So the initial sight—the realization that "I am That"—was present, but other things developed at a later time. When I look back, I realize that what I'm doing now couldn't have happened years ago because there wasn't the clarity. Ultimately, that sense of separation—as though objects are out *there* and the seer is in *here*—dissipates, and all that is left is unicity. All that's left is the love affair. There's no individual anymore, there's simply "this," the beloved. And there's no need to look for anything; the questions are over, and you are simply in love with "what is." Along with this liberation you may occasionally contract back into a sense of separation, but you accept these temporary periods, knowing that all of this is only the manifestation of consciousness.

Liberation isn't a fixed state; it embraces everything and anything. Anger, sadness, and thoughts can still be present, but they all arise in what I am, which is awareness. So, go on hearing the message that you're helpless. Go on listening to people who give you no help at all and who leave you with nothing. A fellow who came to one of my talks said, "Tony, you must teach me how to make money out of selling 'nothing!'"

Go on feeling that helplessness, that longing, and just let it be present. That's the asking, the knocking on the door. And when the door opens, you will realize there never was a door. When you give up, there is the beloved; the beloved is always there. There's no way anyone in this room can avoid "what is." You are the divine expression; everything is the divine expression. There's no need ever to try reaching it because wherever you are, there is always the beloved.

I don't usually speak a lot. In London, I just say a few words and people ask questions. So if anyone wants to ask anything, please go ahead.

Questioner: *Would you clarify what you mean by "pure awareness" and "consciousness."*

Tony Parsons: Awareness is the source of all. As the matrix of everything, it is completely still, silent, and impersonal. It has no relationship with anything; it's the singularity from which everything emanates. Consciousness for me is the soup, which contains anything that *apparently* happens, including the sense of separation. It's whatever arises in consciousness, including the illusion that there's the divine "out there" as well as the feeling "I'm not so divine" in here. Awareness simply is and requires nothing; consciousness can only arise in awareness. Awareness allows this room to be here. There's only this hall; there's only "this." Nothing exists outside this room. When these *apparent* people walk out of this *apparent* hall, there will *apparently* arise a corridor and a bookstore.

Strictly speaking, there is only awareness. All that we see created is consciousness playing the game of hide and seek, creating duality, the illusion of separation. In *The Gospel of Thomas*, Christ says, "When the two become one, we will enter the Kingdom of Heaven." Confusion arises in the drama of life when we think we need time to overcome our sense of separation. Forget it! There's nowhere to go and nothing to attain because this is it.

Questioner: *Is there a practice to help us get close to "this"?*
Tony: Some people will listen and others will hear. The whole idea that there is a "me" who can move toward the destruction of "me" is a fallacy. There is no "me" within nor are there any "me's" without. But the belief in a "me" reinforces the idea that I can improve myself through effort. The truth is, there are no practices to achieve this. If you come to a retreat with Tony Parsons, there's no formality at all. There is no question of creating a time for silence. "Who" is going to be silent? Whatever is, is. It is all the beloved saying, "Come home." At retreats, you're almost guaranteed to be enlightened, and if you are, you have to pay double the fee. [laughter] The whole question of a "me" attempting to practice something to reach what already exists creates the difficulty. You are the divine expression; you are That. This is it—simple awareness. Just know this awareness, which is watching the game of consciousness. You have always been That. There is no need to purify yourself, drop something, or refrain from sinning,

which is really boring. In fact, I'm sinning most of the time.

Questioner: *From your experience, what is the purpose of participating in the world of illusion and dabbling in this drama?*

Tony: There's nothing you can do about it—you've already joined the club! You're in the drama. All that needs to be discovered is that there isn't anyone there, and the drama keeps happening on its own. It's as simple as that; it's as close as that. Drop the idea that there's anyone in the drama. You don't suffer, since there's no one to undergo suffering. There is just suffering. You don't do anything; you've never done anything. You are a character that consciousness plays through. Of course, you have characteristics that are "your" characteristics. I have characteristics that are Tony Parsons' characteristics. I'm obviously intelligent and good-looking, and some people say quite sexy, really [*laughter*]. It's a game; it's a game called "Tony Parsons." Consciousness is Tony Parsonsing. Consciousness is walling, consciousness is speaking, and consciousness is everything that is. You are the awareness that allows all this to be. You are the source of this drama, whose only meaning is to invite you to discover that you are That. You can't stop the drama; you can only let it go on. Just discover that you aren't "living" a life, you *are* life. It's flowing through you—just see it arising and falling away. Emotions and thoughts arise and fall away. So what? They are not you. You are the awareness that allows them and everything else to be.

Questioner: *If consciousness manifests as all that is, is there any value to this illusion?*

Tony: None at all. But it's "what is." It's the game created from the beginning of time, before time began. We are all one, but we had a committee meeting and decided to play the game of two. But in the committee meeting, although we all agreed that we would play this game, we also knew that some of us would forget. So we decided that everything would be an invitation to return home. We also agreed that there would be some people who would remember and tell the others. So, "Hi."

Questioner: Jesus said, "Physician heal thyself." What are your thoughts on healing?

Tony: There isn't anything to heal, really. But until we recognize this, we will attempt to heal what we believe is problematic or not right. Actually, there aren't any problems, nor is there anything that isn't right. Disease is what is; old age is what is. There isn't anyone who "owns" these experiences. This understanding brings with it total poverty and real humility. Humility doesn't mean a person feels less or smaller than someone else. Real humility can only come about when there is no one. True poverty means that we own nothing because there isn't a "me" to own anything. So we don't own ill health or good health; there is just health and ill health. I can't speak about what's commonly called healing. However, I think that possibly the most powerful healing comes about when there is no investment in healing, when there is simply present awareness. Presence is worth a thousand years of good works; it's endless and priceless. One moment of presence lifts the whole world that we believe exists.

Questioner: *Then what is the purpose of doing good works or living a good life, of being just or trying to find an authentic path, if all this doesn't mean anything? How can I find direction is such a world?*

Tony: Good works and direction matter only as long as there is an individual, as long as there's a sense of separation and a belief that there is a path leading somewhere. Such an individual attempts to move along a spiritual path, when in fact there's nowhere to go. All such paths are meaningless. This insight serves as an invitation to fall in love with "what is." When you came to this Gathering, you expected that somehow it would lift you up. Actually, you experience the beloved as you walk into the hall. The steps you take up the stairs or across the hall—that is the beloved. Our attempt to find what we long for—the beloved—is so rich. The history of our attempts to find what we already are is staggering. The richness and the complications in the tradition of searching is something I can't even begin to comprehend. The individual tries to discover something mysterious that is beyond his or her capability to know. There's nothing you can do about *apparently* doing good. If consciousness wants to express itself this way, that's what's going to happen. Just come to see that "this is it." Be ready to jump into whatever is here now and let all else fall away. When you awaken, it's possible that you will still go on living the same sort of life; in fact, most people do. Your life may not change dramatically. You still have to pay income tax and shop for groceries. All those things go on, but your perception will be totally transformed.

Questioner: *Several years ago I had an experience in which I felt that I was "home." There was no place to go; everything was here. After a few days, I felt separateness again, and the difference between the two states was like night and day. I'm filled with longing to realize this again; longing is all I know now. Could you please comment on this?*

Tony: This is very difficult. I'm sure there are a number of people in this room who are familiar with this situation. People have so-called experiences where, for a moment, there is no "me," and they see "I am That." The difficulty arises when there isn't complete clarity about it because they believe that somehow their ego, their unworthiness, has pushed this seeing away. Actually, that isn't how it is. The glimpse is there just for the time it needs to be there—as a glimpse. And when we apparently contract into a state of its absence, that is also the invitation. Nothing has happened, nothing's gone wrong, nor have you done anything incorrectly. You can't push away what you already are; all that's taken place is the glimpse. And if there's clarity, you see that the contraction is also absolutely okay. It's fine; it's part of the invitation. There isn't anything that *isn't* the invitation, so nothing is lost. There is nothing you can do to retrieve the experience, so give up trying and realize that "all there is is this, as it is." Simply come back to the awareness, see *this*, and it will expand and take you over.

Questioner: *The first time I read your book, I didn't understand a word of it, and that was really a great thing for me. My heart would beat really fast, and I could definitely feel myself resonating with the words in body and spirit. After the sixth reading, I was finally able to put the book down. With each reading, I felt that a veil of forgetfulness was lifting. Even* *though I've never had that experience before, there was something familiar about it all. That's one of the reasons I'm here today.*

Tony: Thank you. The words are just words, but when you were reading, something resonated in you with a recognition that comes from a place far deeper than the mind. We all have this wisdom, and all we have to do is recognize it. In England and elsewhere, though in England especially, we share this message with people as friends. When they begin opening up, others come and listen to this guy telling them that they're absolutely helpless to awaken through any personal effort, process, or belief. And they pay money to hear this. [laughter] In this way, people drop their sense of separation and awaken. When awakening happens, they realize that it's the closest thing—and so obvious. This is so obvious; why doesn't everybody just get it? When we read a book, we might think that there are just words on a page, but some sentences jump out at you from the book and penetrate right to your core where you already know "I am That."

Questioner: *I would like to hear you speak about choice and free will. My experience is that I am not choosing to do what I do, but that it is being done. Although it seems like I made a decision to come here, it doesn't seem to resonate fully with me, since the decision really came in an impersonal manner.*

Tony: Having no choice is as much a concept as having absolute choice; they're both concepts. The truth is beyond conceptualization. The mind looks at things from an individual point of view and says, "Have I got a choice?" However, insight reveals that there is no one to make a choice. There is no choice, nor is there free will, simply because there isn't an individual. Only "apparent" choice is being lived through that body/mind by consciousness. We could say that consciousness is the chooser, but until it is seen by "no one" that there is "no one," then just go on choosing—or apparently choosing. Perhaps in your case, much of this is already dropping away. In the end, whatever you choose doesn't matter because you're in the arms of the beloved, no matter what happens.

Questioner: *I hear the words, "we are one," "we are all the divine," "we are all God." So why did we have a committee meeting and agree to be separate individuals, to forget our true nature, only to try to remember it again? Why do we need to relearn or remember if we already know?*

Tony: We don't need to remember since we are already That. Only when the sense of being a separate individual emerges do we feel that there is something to learn. All you're actually learning is that there is nothing to learn. But why not? It's a good game.

Questioner: *If we exist inseparably from God and God knows all, why are we here? Why do we need to reconnect with the source?*

Tony: God knows nothing. God doesn't need to know anything. There is no God separate from you. There is only "what is." Knowledge has nothing to do with this love affair. It simply is like this. Just jump.

Questioner: *Okay, then let me ask it another way. [laughter] In my existence as God, why did I need to take physical form?*
Tony: God hasn't taken physical form. There aren't any physical forms here; there are only *apparent* physical forms. There's only awareness manifesting as an illusion until you see that there is "no me," and then you perceive the real. All this remains unreal as long as there is separation because what you are seeing is unreal. You see separation between that and this, which is unreal. After awakening, you see the real. Again, all I can say to you is that you, who are God, decided in your oneness to become two in order to play the game of feeling separate and becoming one again.

Questioner: *Why?*
Tony: It's great, I tell you! I really recommend it. [laughter]

Questioner: *In asking this question, I realize that I'm speaking conceptually and you're speaking from presence, but I have a question to be asked in two different ways. First, if awareness expresses itself as this room, and what we both apparently see is "what is," how then, when you stay here and I go outside, does my "what is" differ from yours? The other part of the*

question is, why do we tend to see life like a film, one frame at a time, rather than as a whole?

Tony: Let me answer the second part of your question because I'll probably forget the first part. Right now you're seeing all; you're seeing the beloved. This is all there is. This is all you need to see. You don't need to see what's going on in Africa. *This* is it. Incidentally, the film which you're playing frame by frame actually expresses and *is* the whole, so you have the same invitation to awaken either way.

Questioner: *Okay, now here's the first question: When I step outside the room, why is my "what is" different from yours?*

Tony: Because that's uniquely *your* invitation. There's no one else in this room . . .

Questioner: *[interrupts] How can it be uniquely my invitation if there's no "me"?*

Tony: While there is no you, there is a unique body/mind that has been created by consciousness. So everything that appears and everything that arises for that body/mind is uniquely its invitation to discover that there is no separation.

Questioner: *But how can we both be awareness and see phenomena differently?*

Tony: It's because of the diversity of consciousness. Everyone in this room sees everything differently, apparently. There isn't anyone here, yet everyone and everything is manifesting differently. That's the richness, the fun, and the joy of the body/mind's world. However, it is the one appearing as the many.

Questioner: *It's confusing.*

Tony: I know. It's a mystery. It's a mystery that's wonderful to behold when it's beheld by "no one."

Questioner: *Mr. Parsons, you continue to say that it doesn't matter what we do. You also say that we don't have a choice. The Bhagavad Gita says that we should never get lost in action or inaction. If you could contain the whole of infinite awareness in a big piece of chocolate, and you had a choice to cut it into pieces and distribute it to everyone in the world, does that matter or not? Would you keep that entire piece of chocolate? If you had the choice to live with this awareness or share it with others, what would you do?*

Tony: I'd definitely keep the chocolate for myself. [laughter] I'm not here to do service because there's no one to perform service for. I wouldn't have the arrogance to think that you're in need of my services. You are the divine expression. How can I give you anything, how can I tell you to do anything, when you are already That. However, I'm going to keep the chocolate. [laughter]

I think we all have a picture of how an awakened being should be, which is to serve others, to be kind and gentle, and to speak and move slowly. It's bullshit.

Questioner: *You keep saying that everything is an invitation, but I'm not clear on its purpose. I also have a question about practice and personal effort. If awareness is our true nature and we're curious about realizing it, what should we do if we don't engage in a specific practice to increase our awareness of it?*

Tony: There's nothing you can do about practice or no practice. If practice is going to take place, then it will. If consciousness chooses to practice through this body/mind, then that's going to happen. For that person, it is completely appropriate and is absolutely the invitation, just as much as getting drunk in the local bar is for Fred, who lives down the road. He has the same invitation in a way that is completely appropriate for him. As far as the invitation is concerned, awareness, which is the source of all, is also the source of unconditional love. So *everything* is divine; everything comes from awareness, from unconditional love. Everything is the beloved, so wherever your awareness rests, it rests on the beloved. There isn't anywhere where the beloved is not. And the beloved is saying, "Come home."

Questioner: *I'm very curious about inquiring into who I am. If I find myself suffering, I might inquire, "Who am I?" If my body hurts, I might inquire, "What is this body? Do I own it or not?"*

Tony: If that's how it is for your body/mind, that's how it is. It's very interesting that you're sitting in this room, listening, but you don't have to do anything. Our exchange is taking place in the world now, in this *apparent* world. The message that's being communicated by no one is happening now, in a very direct way. So walk out of here, practice and be curious, if that's how it's going to be for you. But also be open to the possibility that just walking up the corridor is it. Just that. The mind has a tendency to think, "When I leave here, I'm going to go meditate, and that's the most important part of the day." Actually, walking out of this room, onto the road, and into the open air is it.

Questioner: There's a refreshing resonance to what you're saying. Your response to chocolate was delightful, but the absence of the need to serve is puzzling, since by your choice you're currently sitting at the front of a room, serving. I'd love for you to comment on why you've made that choice when there's no one to serve.

Tony: It's mainly for the money, really. [laughter] I've sold used cars before, but this seems like a better job.

Questioner: I just want to say that I think you're very sexy. But I also have a question. I had an experience about twelve years ago much like your "walking across the park." It seemed to endure for a deliciously long time. And since that time, it's almost unbearably more difficult to avoid being caught in the story and the drama, the children and the relationship. Do we just get one glimpse? It's really hard not to chase the experience.

Tony: I understand. After the "walking across the park," it was, in a way, like a curse for a while, because somehow I felt that something was lost. I know this can be a very difficult place to be, because psychological difficulties or fears may arise, which are seen by the watcher. These nearly always arise at some point or other.

The critical period feels like a desert experience. At this point, people lose or drop all their values about life. However, there has not been a falling in love with "this." They find themselves in the desert, the wilderness where Christ was tested. And it's very interesting to observe how some people in that desert listen to the devil (I'm being very religious now), and they return to the security of what they "know." Because the mind wants something to catch hold of that it can know and do, people often run back to old structures of thought where they feel safe.

Questioner: *I like what you're saying—most of it, I think.*
Tony: No, you have to like all of it. [laughter]

Questioner: *I struggle with bringing this truth to my children. I can grasp it for myself and take responsibility for making it part of my life. But when I look at my two beautiful teenage daughters, I wonder how to bring them into this truth. I can't envision telling them, "It's all right to pass by the homeless; don't worry about giving them money because there is nothing you can add to this already divine life." This is what I struggle* *with. Could you please address this?*

Tony: You are helpless in reacting and responding to anyone else in the world. Whatever happens takes place in its own way. It's reassuring to know that whatever happens for your *apparent* children will be the perfect invitation uniquely presented for them. It's difficult to attempt to help others when there is still a sense of separation, especially when there is very little clarity about yourself.

This is really a "do or die" situation. Either there is light or there is apparent darkness. If there is apparent darkness, if there is confusion, then you can only do your best and know that somewhere your children are held by the beloved. You just have to follow the obvious—whatever your education is, whatever your religion happens to be, etc. There is nothing you can do about that; you're helpless. That's the way it's going to be until everything falls away, and there's no longer anything but "this." Then whatever happens is spontaneous and clear.

Questioner: *I feel the conflict between loving God, the beloved, which seems to arise spontaneously in me, and the strong feeling "I am That." The conflict creates a duality between* loving *that and* being *that.*

Tony: Yes, thank you for that. These days I see quite a lot of difficulty in people who are moving away from the limited sense of "me" and are moving into an awareness of That. However, they are confused about the apparent identity that carries this awareness. As a gentleman at this Gathering said, "Walking out of the hall appears to this identity, so is there still a 'me' there?" In fact, there isn't, but somewhere the penny hasn't dropped. A greater awareness is taking place, but the mind still has a sense of the identity that it carries around. Until the last penny drops, it can be a bit confusing. And again, you're helpless anyway, so it's going to be fine. It's fine now.

Questioner: Tony, I have a couple of questions. In the workshops that you give, where no people come and nothing is done, could you describe what the non-people don't do when they don't do anything? The second question is simpler: You walked across the courtyard and the non-describable happened. Could you take a stab at using words to describe the indescribable?

Tony: Really, people who come to retreats and workshops aren't doing anything. Nothing is happening differently than going down the road and buying fish and chips. We just happen to be in a room together sharing words and a resonance. To some extent, however, when two or three gather together, a powerful resonance does take place. But I always say to people, "When you walk out of this hall, get in your car and go home, just be open to the reality that is there as well." It's not just here; there's nothing special or sacred about this. Everything is sacred; everything is the invitation. So in the workshops where no one is doing anything, there is only the appearance of doing something, but none of it has any meaning.

The first glimpse of reality is the most staggering of all because something atomic happens. There is no longer a "me," but only "this." The feeling "I am That" is quite near, and we touch an unconditional love that is lived completely when it is fully seen that there is truly no one there. That first glimpse is astonishing for the person who is living in apparent darkness. The light permeates everything with unconditional love. Thereafter, as far as Tony Parsons is concerned, the glimpses or openings that followed the initial one never had quite the same impact. Even though the light had initially dissipated the apparent darkness, a residue still existed. Ultimately, that went away. Now there aren't any questions, nothing is missing, and there is only this love affair.

The mind wants to look for an event, such as walking across the park or walking down the road, but this is it, right here and now.

Questioner: Since you've been talking, I've been in panic because I've had some openings and closings, and I've created an expectation about what has to happen next. I realize that "This is it," yet I've developed a fear and resistance about going back in the apparent darkness. Can you give me some pointers to deal with the fearful emotions that come up around this issue?

Tony: Whatever emotion comes up is "what is." When we live in separation, the mind tends to get hold of these sensations and turn them into stories. The last thing the mind wants to do is to let emotions simply be present, to be seen by the watcher, which is pure awareness. It wants to possess that emotion and turn it into a story that will convince you that the mind will work out the problem and somehow find a solution. Instead, simply rest in "what is," whether it is the taste of marmalade or tea, the emotion of fear, or the noise of a car going by. All these apparent happenings are simply consciousness manifesting the invitation in every form. So let those things be as they are by simply seeing it all with awareness. It's very simple. Christ said that the kingdom of heaven is like a mustard seed. It is tiny and ordinary, and is arising as "this."

Questioner: Earlier, you mentioned that when two or more are gathered, a powerful resonance can happen. I'm curious about the relation between intention and openness. Is there intention when two or more are gathered?

Tony: There is *apparent* intention, but this intention has no connection with openness. Intention is a motivation or energy. People may come to these meetings holding on to the motivation of finding something. But what manifests in these meetings is the sense of spaciousness. If there is total absence of the "me" as a body/mind, then those who feel separate expand into that spaciousness and resonate with it. The sense of non-separation leads to the resonance that takes place "when two or more gather."

Questioner: Is the invitation and intention part of the game?

Tony: Everything is part of the game. Consciousness is all there, all that manifests. The invitation is in everything that manifests, but is connected with the idea of being an individual who can move toward a goal. Intention is about motive.

Questioner: *You've spoken a few times about dropping the sense of separation. If I look at my experience right now, there is definitely an experience of separation in it. But I can't understand the point of dropping it. It's only a sense, after all, like the sense of sight. I regard the ego as a kind of sense organ that we humans have, which creates this sense of separation. But if I try to drop it, I simply can't, nor do I really see a problem with it. And "who" would drop it anyway? Plus, why give the ego so much validity?*

Tony: That's lovely. Since everything we're talking about is conceptual, let your separation be there, if that's how it is for your body/mind. You haven't got any problems, so rejoice in your separation!

Conclusion

We've been speaking quite a bit. There's no need to get into the lotus position. You can close your eyes or keep them open. See whether it's possible to just "drop" the person who's been walking around with you all these years, the one who tries to work it out, making judgments and calculations. You don't need that person, nor do you need boundaries. Just get a sense of being free of all boundaries, of being no-thing. You are simply awareness, seeing whatever arises. It's absolutely simple, and it's absolutely what you are. Just let awareness see what arises. And don't give what arises any identity. Just allow it to be—as it is—without any recognition or identity; don't try and work it out or control it.

CHAPTER TWO

Tustin
Unity Church

"What you seek is
closer to you than your
own breath."

T hank you for coming here. I just want to say before we go any further that I'm not an enlightened person. For me, there's no such thing as an "enlightened person." Nobody in this room will ever become enlightened. The difficulty that we have is that when we're young, we're taught that we have to achieve something, to attain something. We're taught how to do well on exams, get good jobs, and get good wives and husbands. Our conditioning focuses on getting and attaining things because we believe that they'll fulfill us.

Well, for quite a lot of *apparent* people—I use the word "apparent" quite a lot—that's all that's necessary, that's all one really needs. Others, however, never find it fulfilling to have a lot of money, good relationships, or the whole list of things that's supposed to make them happy. No matter how they fill the list, it isn't fulfilling. They feel there must be something else beyond all that, and for many people one of the answers is therapy. People think about going to a therapist to work through their issues and to practice self-improvement. Because therapy seems to be the answer to our problems, we often try this body method and that affirmation technique. They seem to work for a few moments or even for a few days, but for some of us that really isn't enough, and we're left unfulfilled.

Then we hear about "enlightenment" and want to find out more about it. People exclaim, "Oh, that person's enlightened!" and they run to see him or her. Then they say, "This new teacher is wonderful," and they flock to see the new person. One of these teachers may tell you, "This is the answer," or "I'm the one." And you go from one person to another, searching for this thing called, "Enlightenment." In all your seeking, you always look "somewhere" for "something" that's outside yourself. This way of looking at enlightenment comes under the same category as looking for a good job, a spouse, or a therapist.

Throughout it all, you're driven by an unfulfilled longing, which the mind turns into an object called enlightenment or awakening. You work to get enlightenment the same way that you put in effort to attain any goal. Strangely enough, enlightenment, awakening, or liberation, never happens this way, and what blocks it from happening is *you*.

The idea that you can attain enlightenment is the veil that continuously keeps it away. Seeking only increases the problem. In fact, seeking is the most effective way of avoiding awakening. The seeker continually promotes the idea that "what is, as it is," isn't it. The seeker says, "This can't be it, it has to be something more, it has to be elsewhere, and the reason that it hasn't happened to me is that I'm not good enough. I never have been good enough. I'm not trying hard enough." The crazy thing is that the harder you try to reach enlightenment, the more you push it away.

We've all heard stories of those wonderful people who sit on mountaintops, meditate for years, and become enlightened. Actually, if you asked them about their awakening and if they were honest and clear, they'd tell you that they had meditated for many years, and at the moment of giving up the idea that there's anything to attain, awakening took place.

There's nothing to attain and nothing to do because what you're seeking is right here now. What you seek is closer to you than your own breath. What you seek has always been the case, so it's with you this very moment. As you sit here, looking at this apparent person named Tony Parsons, something within you sees you looking at him. This something is your original nature, what you really are, and has nothing to do with the individual you think you are. You have funny knobby bits, like neurosis and worry, a spouse, and all the things you believe make up your individuality. Rather than being what you are, these are just creations manifesting.

You are the one who sees it all, knows it all, and watches all that is happening. You are the still, silent source of all that is, the Being that animates the body/mind, the Being in which everything arises, including the apparent individual. That

Being, that awareness, is what you are.

You're not a part of the whole, but the *source* of the whole. Because you are, everything else is. Whatever we see, whatever we think is our life story, whatever we believe the world to be is only an appearance of Being and unconditional love. There's no world out there; there's only Being and unconditional love appearing as the invitation to drop the sense of "me," to drop the idea that there's any separation, to drop the idea that there's any individual sitting in this room. There's only Being, living in and as every apparently different body/mind.

In the drama of creation, we have a longing to discover the truth that "I am absolute Being." When awakening happens, the mystery reveals itself as something quite ordinary. There aren't great fireworks or lights. I don't see anything different than you see. What's different is that there's no one looking anymore. And so life goes on, but not as some extraordinary, amazing, or problem-free existence.

After awakening, you don't live in total bliss. The idea of living in total bliss is an aberration of the mind, a misguided teaching that has no basis in reality. Bliss has nothing to do with awakening. While there are moments of blissfulness, awakening unfolds in ordinary and natural ways, and we see life and existence as they really are.

In separation, we see the unreal, separate world. In awakening, we see that everything emanates from the source, which is unconditional love.

The other part of this message is that there's absolutely nothing you can do about hastening or slowing down awakening. You could not have done anything differently because no one can *do* anything. Since there's nowhere to go, how can you move toward something? Everything that you apparently did in your lifetime as a body/mind has been absolutely perfect. You could never have done otherwise because you weren't doing it. Presence lives through your body/mind at all times. We all have our own perfect, unique invitation at every moment, and for the rest of our apparent life things will continue like that. Presence will always live through you, extending to you the total invitation.

Grace doesn't float around in the sky and shoot arrows at the worthy. You live in constant grace. Since there isn't one moment when you aren't in grace, you're constantly being invited to see that you're the source. Knowing this, you need never come to meetings anymore! You're always in a meeting, you're always being held, you're always being invited, and you're always in love. You can't escape being in love, but you can think that you're unloved. Actually, not only are you *in* love, but you *are* love itself; you are the very source of love.

What I'm talking about is simplicity itself—accepting the invitation, letting go, and being very intimate with whatever arises, including your thoughts. Some people tell you that you need to stop thinking, to drop your ego, and to eliminate desire. Such an approach is completely ridiculous because there's *no one* there to do it. And, as you already know, we've all tried!

You've most likely read that being here now is the answer. Have you seen the lovely cartoon in which a girl looks at the mirror and says, "Well, tomorrow morning I'm going to start 'being here now'"? We've all read these things, and for a time the mind thinks, "This is wonderful, it's the answer to all my problems. I'm not going to think anymore!"

This resolution may last for at least an hour, which is pretty good, actually. Instead of such imposed effort, why not see that what you long for is already the case? You can't do anything about it because it already is the case.

How can I tell you how you should be when you're already divine? Every one of you *is* the divine expression, just as you are, uniquely as you are—no better, no worse, because you are That. Of course, once this falling in love happens, you fall in love with yourself. All that's happening here is that you're listening to yourself, and when you meet others, you're meeting yourself in the form of Bill, Mary, or whoever it is. It's as simple as that.

Everyone lives in meditation; everyone takes part in this process. Every apparent person in existence shares in the invitation and in the process, which doesn't lead to a destination like a path. It's simply "this"—always the invitation.

When I first began speaking to people, I didn't actually say anything. I used to sit on a chair for twenty minutes. After some awkward movements, people would ask questions, which led to a conversation among friends. Because this is a conversation among friends, I talk to people in this introductory manner just to break the ice.

Questioner: *What you're saying is plain and simple, but I've*

never heard it put that way. Is there a right or wrong way to this approach?

Tony: No one can live the way I'm speaking about because no one is even there to do it! Open yourself to the revolutionary realization that no one is sitting there. No one has ever chosen anything, nor can anyone do so. Whatever's going to happen will happen, regardless of the person you think exists. The idea that there's anyone there is a total illusion, a wisp of smoke. Everything you do, everything that happens through your body/mind is totally and perfectly appropriate. So give up the idea that there's a right way you "should" behave. Exactly the way you move and talk is the divine expression. Whatever ideas your mind might have about right or wrong are illusory concepts.

Questioner: *What you're saying sounds almost too simple. What surprises me is that I'm unable to intellectually grasp the essence. Does this mean that my mind doesn't have the proper ability?*

Tony: It means that what you are is completely beyond the mind and that it will never understand what we are talking about here. I suggest that you not listen exclusively to the words being spoken. We all have knowledge and wisdom that is far deeper than the mind can ever reach. We all possess intuitive wisdom that can jump over walls the mind can never scale.

What's being said is totally understood by no one because there's no one sitting here. While the mind can never understand this, something else within each of us is completely saying "yes" to this message. In this kind of meeting, apparent people come in with concepts about what enlightenment is and how they hope to achieve it. Perhaps some of them will leave with their concepts destroyed. They'll go home, then, with absolutely nothing!

Questioner: *So why is it that we don't "understand"? Why is there this apparent ignorance?*

Tony: You started it. You may pretend to be Bill, but you're really pure awareness and total stillness manifesting as Bill, experiencing the separation from paradise. Consciousness chose to play the game of the one manifesting as two in separation in order to rediscover itself as the one. In the Gospel of Thomas, Christ says, "When you make the two one, you will enter the Kingdom of Heaven." In a way, I quite envy you because awakening is so wonderful. You persist in staying separate because you find it fascinating. Yet awakening is inevitable, and when it happens, it will be wonderful. Only then will you see why you were so "ignorant" before.

Questioner: *When did this awakening happen for you and what led to it?*

Tony: It didn't happen to "me." The "me" that was apparently there dropped away. Nothing actually happens in awakening because it's already the case. Everything begins as pure light, and then we fall into the illusion of being a "me" who can't find the light. We *are* the light. We're like a fish in the ocean that is looking for water. When we awaken, the illusion of "me" drops away, and what remains is "already the case."

Questioner: *I started as a psychotherapist but found that psychological work wasn't enough, so I became a massage therapist. Now that I've been in contact with you and others from the nondual tradition, I'm beginning to see that I'm not the mind or the body. I find that my work with patients has lost its once-solid basis. From the perspective of Being, is my work really useless?*

Tony: Nothing that manifests has any meaning at all. Whatever we think is what we do. However, we aren't really doing anything, since consciousness does everything through us. Whatever we think we're doing will never lead anywhere because there's nowhere to go. We aren't in a linear story that's progressing toward a better condition. Right now we're in paradise; this is paradise. We're motivated to do things because they attract us, because we hope they'll improve us, and because we wish to help others, but such actions are totally without meaning. On the other hand, your body/mind can't do anything about doing massage or not doing it. If that's what's going to happen, it will go on happening.

Each of us has a unique invitation to awaken. When your "me" totally drops away, you can still go on doing massage, but with a completely different perception. Some people's lives change outwardly, but for most, they go on as they did before, except that they have a tremendous sort of freedom. You no longer have an investment in trying to help others because there aren't others to help. You enjoy and feel intimate with whatever arises. Give up the idea that you must do something to prove your worthiness as a good therapist, parent, or spouse. Such efforts stem from the mind trying to discover meaning where, in fact, there is none.

Questioner: If the only thing here is consciousness and there's no one present, then who can accept the invitation? Isn't this a paradox: to find the person who can accept, yet there's no one here?

Tony: No person can accept the invitation. Actually, when the invitation is accepted, the mind simply gives up. In most cases, the answer people get turns them back on themselves where they find that there's no one there and nothing to get. There's nothing you can do, even though the mind always says, "Don't worry, I can work all this out for you."

Questioner: Is it possible to stop the mental noise, since there's no one here to surrender?

Tony: No, there's no one to surrender, nor is there anything to be surrendered, because what's apparently surrendered is only an illusion anyway. It's a mystery that the mind can never comprehend, yet the mind will go on convincing you that it can.

Although whatever happens is absolutely perfect and appropriate, the mind wants to turn that into a process. It will say, for example, "Let's go home and *do* nothing now," instead of allowing the mind to come back to "what is" in its simplicity. Just sitting in your seat is the beloved, and this is the invitation to come home. If you're in close contact with the beloved you'll hear the invitation as a shout, and it's possible to drop the sense of "me" in that deep intimacy.

When you leave here today, get in your car and drive home. If you realize that you're in the arms of the beloved and you stay intimate with ordinary things, the adventure can begin.

Questioner: *What if we have a goal like going to college or changing careers? These things require decisions, like the decision to come here today. How did you decide to come here?*
Tony: Actually, I didn't. I don't make decisions anymore. My wife said that we're coming. As far as choices are concerned, if you still have the sense of being an individual, then it's okay to go on choosing. Live as though you choose, but begin opening to the realization that *you* are actually not choosing anything.

You can't stop choosing to take a medical degree or become an artist. If it's going to happen, it will just happen. After awakening, of course, it no longer matters, and in the state of true liberation, you can become anything. Of course, you will work and communicate in ways that come naturally to you.

Questioner: *Are you saying, then, that things just evolve?*
Tony: Yes, they evolve, but at the same time nothing happens at all. Since nothing has any meaning, the ideas we have about work and relationships are illusions. You can only do your best as long as you have a sense of being an individual. Only then can you follow what you believe is the best path. Why not begin moving into the adventurous possibility that nothing has any meaning? Unconditional love is totally neutral; it doesn't lean towards goodness and try to avoid evil.

As far as the Absolute is concerned, everything in this apparent world that we live in is absolutely neutral. Whatever apparent good happens, which we tend to call "spiritual," is equally balanced by what we perceive as evil. Positive and negative are always perfectly balanced so that everything is totally neutral.

Questioner: *What about feelings such as nervousness? How do they relate to the fact that there is no one here?*

Tony: Feelings simply happen; they don't belong to anyone who is nervous. Saying "I'm nervous" reinforces the idea that there's someone there. Instead, just say, "There is nervousness," and you've begun to have a totally different perception. No one is ever nervous or angry. Anger happens here, but there is no one angry. I own nothing, I am nothing; there's no one here. This is Christ's real teaching about poverty. Total poverty means that there is no ownership of anything including suffering, anger, or nervousness, which simply arise. Whenever a feeling such as nervousness arises in awareness, be intimate with it, knowing "who" is feeling anything.

Questioner: *How can one bring about the acceptance of nothingness?*

Tony: You can't *do* anything about it because it's just going to happen. If you're sitting here listening to this, then something is ready to hear. There's no one in this room. There's just life happening in this body/mind and this awareness, which is the source of everything that arises in it. But no one's here and life's just unfolding. You don't have a life; you've never had a life; you *are* life.

Questioner: *A few minutes ago you said that paradise is here. What do you mean by that? Do I need a new definition of paradise?*

Tony: You don't need anything. Once you're not here, there's only paradise. You're the problem. When you drop the idea that there's a "you" looking for paradise, everything flowers as unconditional love—the walls, the chairs, and also the drama of separation.

You are unconditional love itself. You're sitting in paradise, believing that it's somewhere else. When you leave, you'll drive in your car through paradise, and when you get home and you're thirsty, you'll drink paradise. You only think or believe otherwise.

Questioner: *Then why are we here in the situation we're in?*
Tony: Why not? There's no one to choose either being here or not being here. The people who aren't here couldn't have done anything about not being here. No one chooses anything.

What I'm communicating here is absolutely direct—nothing hidden at all. Interestingly, more and more people are ready to hear this message, undiluted as it is.

Questioner: *If that's the case, do our actions have any meaning at all?*
Tony: No, none at all. Life has no purpose, and that's the beauty of it. Life isn't trying to get anywhere or do anything. We're brought up to believe that we've got to get somewhere and do something, that life has meaning, and that God must have done all this for us. The truth is, there's no God nor are there separate people. There's only love. There's only light, which doesn't need to go anywhere. Why should it need to go anywhere? This is paradise.

The world isn't going to get better or worse. We're not going to save the world because it doesn't need saving. Since we live in a neutral world, it's always going to be like this, which only has one message: Come home, awaken, you are the light.

Questioner: *Someone who's changed my life has three concepts. The first two are, "All there is is consciousness" and "Events happen and deeds are done, but there's no individual doer." I was fine with these two, but somehow I couldn't link it with the third, which is "Nothing happens unless it's the will of God." The last part blew my world apart.*

Tony: What was your problem with the "will of God"?

Questioner: *Personally, I had a very polarized view of God. God was practically sitting on my shoulder and could do no wrong. If things happened in the world that were "wrong," it was because we have free will and were making the error.*

Tony: There is no God, and there is no will. The idea that everything is the will of God reinforces the sense that the manifestation is going somewhere, that somehow there's still someone out there who's running things.

Questioner: *So that, too, is dualistic. There is no "Thy will"?*

Tony: No, that's absolutely dualistic.

Questioner: *This particular teacher talks about "Thy will" a lot, and you're saying that there's no "Thy."*

Tony: That's right. There's no one there and no will to be done. The only will that exists is "this." So there's no succession of events with one thing and then another. All of this is simply the light, the divine expression, which is totally fixed and still. We think of the world as something moving, like a series of flashing photographs, but it's actually one still expression of love. When Nisargadatta said, "Nothing is happening," that's what he meant. Actually, nothing *ever* happens.

Questioner: *What about the concept of predestination?*
Tony: Oh, no, that's a mental concept. There's no such thing as destiny, which implies movement toward somewhere. There isn't anywhere to go; this is it.

Questioner: *Whatever happens is moment by moment?*
Tony: It's only apparently happening to the mind, the entity that needs the invitation. Once the invitation is accepted, there's nothing left but simply "this."

Questioner: *What about cause and effect in relationships? The law of cause and effect is in almost all the scriptures.*
Tony: As long as you have the sense of being a separate individual, you'll believe in cause and effect. And your mind will find evidence to prove that there's such a thing as cause and effect. It's the same with karma, reincarnation, good and evil. As long as an apparent individual believes in a separate world, that belief will create what seems to be cause and effect. When you accept the invitation, you'll discover that something lies beyond what apparently happens, including the concepts of cause and effect, karma and separation.

It's as if all the apparent events of life are being projected on a movie screen. I say "apparent" because the light has to discover that it's the light that allows the film to play. Once we make that discovery, we see that the sense of cause and effect, karma, is an hypnotic dream that loses any meaning. We then come back to the realization that "this is it." Nothing needs to happen for this realization to take place. This always is it. In three years' time, it will be the same.

Questioner: Do you not believe in reincarnation or past lives?
Tony: No one reincarnates. No one has a past life because there's no one. There never has been anyone. Isn't this amazing? In the whole of creation, in the whole history of this world, there never has been anyone.

Questioner: Why does the mind stop us from accepting the invitation to come home?
Tony: Because this is the drama that the source, which you are, created in order to enjoy this manifestation in all its diversity. Look at all the colors and all the different apparent people in this room, all with their own characteristics. And look at all the different ways in which people try to discover what they are. It's a wonderful, wonderful game. When awakening takes place, we have a love affair with everything in diversity. Give up asking why.

Questioner: How does the mind do this?
Tony: Consciousness uses the mind to create this room, which is only a thought form. The mind creates this manifestation.

Questioner: You say that there's no universal meaning to anything. But in a deeper sense, it seems that everything does have meaning.

Tony: When we accept the invitation, we awaken to the is-ness of everything, which has no meaning, but is simply, "I am That." We have a love affair in which the is-ness is seeing, the being-ness is seeing "I am That." But life has no meaning, nor is it heading anywhere. It doesn't need to go anywhere because *this* is the love affair, this is paradise, and "I am That."

Questioner: Our dualistic mind runs from pain and toward pleasure. How do you experience something painful like an injury? Is there an experience without an evaluation of it?

Tony: That's it.

Questioner: So when pain arises, it just arises, and there's no evaluation of it? Or if pleasure or joy arises, it's just there?

Tony: I think "evaluation" may not be quite the word. To be clearer, I would say there's no personal investment in it; there is just "what is."

Questioner: Let's say that while you're watching a movie, someone in the movie is hurt and you feel for that person. The injury isn't happening to your body. Is your experience something like this?

Tony: To me the taste of tea, anger, emotions, or intuitive feelings about someone are all the same. And incidentally, you don't have to *watch* a film; everything *is* a film.

Questioner: *When I'm in a good place and free of anxiety, I open to all this and it resonates with me. But when I feel pain, I don't. I don't feel "neutral," and something within me wants to change it.*

Tony: You won't ever feel neutral as long as there's a "you." True neutrality arises in no one and is apparent to no one.

Questioner: *My mind is going . . .*

Tony: The mind is going mad because it doesn't get it. It doesn't want to get it. It can't sit on the throne anymore. Whose throne is it going to sit on?

Questioner: *I'm having trouble translating this into everyday life. For example, I was sitting in my office yesterday with a mother who was absolutely repulsed by her daughter and couldn't love her, even though it's what the daughter needed. If I were to tell the mother, "You know everything is perfect, even being repulsed by your daughter and not being able to stand her," I wouldn't be painting a pretty picture.*

Tony: No. No one said anything about existence being beautiful or perfect. Whatever is arising is perfectly appropriate, but it's not perfect in the sense that the mind thinks of as perfect. And it's not beautiful that she doesn't like her daughter. It's what is.

Generally, because we live in separation, we avoid everyday, ordinary life, hoping to find something around the corner that's bigger and "better" than what is. Instead, let's learn to be totally and intimately alive with just "this," from which arises spontaneous action and unconditional love.

I can't suggest what you should say to the mother because I never tell anybody to act a certain way. How can I? Everybody already *is* the divine expression.

Questioner: I understand what you're saying, but when she walks out of my office, if I've expressed to her what you've been saying, she'll continue being repulsed by her daughter, and there will be mutual suffering. In the grand scheme of things, it really doesn't matter, but on the level of love and compassion, it does.
Tony: No, it doesn't. The level that the mind understands to be love and compassion is only a faint reflection of the love and compassion of awakening—a love that's so radiant it would blow your mind. This total, unconditional love, which accepts and embraces everything, is liberation.

Questioner: If that mother could get a taste of such love, it might enable her to change.
Tony: Of course, it would, but there's nothing you can do about it. You can never really help another, you only apparently help by doing your best. No matter what's happening, you have no responsibility for anyone because there's no you, nor is there anybody else, either. Manifestation is a film upon which is projected a game called the hypnotic dream-world full of individuals. In truth, there are no individuals, nor is there anyone to help.

Questioner: When I picture myself saying this to her, I see her rejecting me and walking out of my office.

Tony: When there's a readiness to say it, your body/mind will say it. Until then, you can only do your best with what you've got.

Questioner: In your book As It Is, *there's something I find problematic, which you call the "be here now concept." Where does the problem arise with "being here now"?*

Tony: What I try to say in the book isn't connected with the idea of "being here now." There isn't anyone who isn't "here now." A book written a number of years ago called *Be Here Now* helped bring to awareness the notion of being in the "now." But there's no such thing as now. Where is now?

Questioner: Aren't the concepts of "now" and "as it is" the same thing?

Tony: In the book, I say that "being here now" is the normal state for people in the hypnotic dream, whether they're dreaming of being in the Bahamas or walking along the road looking for shoes. In either case, they're hypnotized in the dream that we might call "now."

Questioner: Why is that an illusion for people who look back on themselves in the moment?

Tony: When we are hypnotized by a dream, we take ourselves to be a person with a separate life, I call this state "being here now." When we awaken, we realize that there's no one to be in the now or any other time.

Questioner: So nobody's focused on looking at himself?
Tony: That's right. Self-observation is generally the mind watching the mind. The mind watches what it thinks is happening, interprets it, and usually judges it in some way or other. Self-observation has no connection with awakening. It's just another activity that happens in the dream of "me."

Questioner: Is awakening somewhat like mindfulness?
Tony: No, it certainly isn't because the Buddhist concept of living mindfully with what's happening involves a subtle sense of someone doing something, which is "mindful-ing." Living in this state of concentrated awareness still subtly reinforces separation.

In the end, awakening lies completely beyond any concept of awareness. There isn't any personal awareness; there's no one to be aware. There's just "this," and "I am That"—a realization which is impossible to describe.

Deep wisdom is knowing that "I am awareness, I am nothing," but unconditional love is knowing that "I am everything." The word love has all sorts of connotations, but the nearest I can get to it is *absolute Being*. When the state of unconditional love is total, it leads to the final realization, "I am absolute Being" or "There's just absolute Being."

Questioner: I hear you say there's not a God, yet you use the words "light," "divine," and "unconditional love." How is that different?
Tony: It isn't.

Questioner: *Are these just semantic differences?*

Tony: It's impossible to express "this"— it is the hardest job there is. Unconditional love, the Absolute, the no-thing, the beloved: these words might appeal or touch one person but not another. They suggest something that's beyond words— the impersonal, the still, silent source, which is what you are. It's impossible to put the source of all into words. If you called it "marmalade," it might be just as good.

Questioner: *You say there's no God, yet you use these other words. Are you saying there's nothing the word "God" points to?*

Tony: There's no one here; there's nothing but awareness. "God," conceived as almighty intelligence, with a will that creates and manages this world, simply doesn't exist. Only energy, love, and light exist. It's even not right for me to say, "You're the source." There's *just* the source, which happens to function through this body/mind. It creates this room and everybody else arising in this unique awareness, but it's all generated from no-thing, from the Absolute. Here we go again, with another list of words. Marmalade.

Questioner: *You said that you see what we see. Essentially, we see a physical form named Tony Parsons. Beyond this form there's an amorphous blob of all-loving consciousness that surrounds us, yet we feel separate from it. I have a closer affinity with my body/mind than with yours. For example, you have*

friends whom I don't know. I don't know what your favorite food is or what your sensations are. When awakening destroys our sense of separateness, how do things change?

Tony: Things don't change; nothing changes except that whatever occurs happens to no one. Things simply happen, apparently. Whatever happens in this body/mind here is no more or less important than what happens in the body/mind there. Nothing is more or less sacred than anything else. As far as knowing what you've had for breakfast is concerned, it's totally irrelevant. What's important is that we see the source manifesting as everything.

These are just words. What's actually happening here goes beyond words and concepts. What I see is "me" arising as That. When I say "me," I don't mean Tony Parsons—here we go with words again! Unconditional love is arising as That; unconditional love is manifesting as the wall, chairs, flowers, and someone named Matthew. Are there any Rogers in the room? [laughter]

It's impossible to communicate this verbally because words lean towards separation. But we all know moments when the little self vanishes into pure presence. We all know this because in reality we *are* That. After the apparent death of the body/mind, nothing, of course, has changed, because there is no birth, only the *appearance* of a body/mind. So there isn't any duration and nothing happens. There's only unconditional love, which manifests and expresses through apparent body/minds. When a body/mind is no more, what remains is unconditional love, because that's all there was anyway.

Death means the end of the illusion of separation, and at the moment of death there's just unconditional love. To put it another way: you come out of your home to play the game of being separate, and at the moment of death, you simply return home.

Questioner: *There must be some reason why all this takes place.*

Tony: Why? I have no idea. You don't have to do anything about it because you're at home in the divine source, which was never born and which will never die. Nothing ever happens except the appearance of an apparent life that lives in an illusory state of separation.

Questioner: *So all this is about death, isn't it?*

Tony: Yes, it's the death of the illusion of "me."

Questioner: *Which is the awakening . . .*

Tony: Yes, everyone becomes awakened by either dying in life or dying at one's apparent death. What dies is the illusion.

Questioner: *Is that where all our fear comes from? Aren't we afraid to let go of something that we believe gives us a sense of identity? Although the "me" ceases to exist, what we really are never dies.*

Tony: Only an illusory sense of self dies, which never had any real existence anyway. We're frightened of the silliest thing of all: the mind fears that it's going to die, when actually it doesn't have any existence anyway. Only an illusion dies.

Questioner: *These fears arise because we think we have to hold on to something, to be something. When we let go and realize that we're nothing, we realize our true existence. I work hard at being a good mother, providing for my family, and maintaining a meaningful relationship.*

Tony: You have to put huge amounts of energy into it.

Questioner: *Not working to achieve enlightenment seems difficult because everything I've learned involves work. How can we stop the mind, which is so active, from doing work to achieve enlightenment?*

Tony: You can't achieve it. When the mind becomes bored with its usual strategies, something else arises.

Questioner: *Do you promise?*

Tony: Ultimately, the mind gives up because there's nowhere for it to go. It's as simple as that. When it just gives up, becomes bored, and realizes its limitations, something else happens. However, let's be careful about this, because it doesn't always happen that way. Awakening has no formula, after all. We can't say that everyone in this room has to exhaust the mind and become bored. It's possible that at a quarter past ten tonight [snaps his fingers] awakening will happen, regardless of the mind's condition.

Questioner: *Would you comment about the power and efficacy, if any, of transmission?*

Tony: Before or after awakening, no one chooses anything. No one can choose to impart any sort of power, and certainly no one can help or push anybody else into enlightenment. Those who insist on the necessity of transmission speak from ignorance or the wish to manipulate others. There's no one here, and I'm not doing anything. I'm not turning on the power, directing it to certain people, or thinking, "This one is a worthy person." I don't play such games. There's no need to do anything since all this is the divine expression.

The energy of no-thing is filling this room. When your body/mind is no longer invested in the idea of separation, a spaciousness arises, and apparent people expand into that space. It happens at meetings like this when two or more are gathered together.

This has nothing to do with a teacher or a charismatic leader. Throughout history, we've projected our hopes of salvation onto others who had "it" and who we expected would give it to us. That's complete nonsense.

Questioner: I understand your message intellectually, but want to incorporate it into my life so that I live in an absolutely perfect way. When I live that way, whatever choice this body/mind makes will be absolutely perfect for me and the body/minds around me, because everything will be an expression of the divine and not of "me."

Tony: Until there's no one there, it will never happen like that. You can't make it happen. As long as you want to shape your behavior, you'll be holding on to a belief. Awakening has absolutely nothing to do with belief, which as a function of the mind impels you to live in a particular manner. When you hold on to and believe in a concept, you empower its opposite, which is doubt. Belief and doubt live together as two sides of the same coin.

Questioner: *But isn't it a state of being?*
Tony: It is, but there's nothing you can do about it because it's already the case. Only your belief that it isn't attained stands in the way. Ideas such as "I haven't got it," "It hasn't happened yet," "It won't happen to me because I was a poor student when I was a kid," or "Everyone else in this room is going to get it, but I won't," hold you back.

You'll never *get* it. No one will ever *get* it because it's already the case.

Questioner: *How does this understanding affect your relationship with your wife?*
Tony: Most of the time we're not really in a "relationship" anymore because I'm fortunate enough to live with someone who isn't anyone.

Questioner: *You're not getting away with that!*
Tony: Let's be clear about something that we haven't talked much about tonight. After awakening, you can still move in and out of awareness. While your perception of "I am That, I am the Absolute, I am awareness, I am the light just as everyone else is" remains constant, in certain circumstances you can still contract back into identification. This means that at times you can still be in a relationship and at other times in a non-

relationship. Both things can happen together. Whichever arises is the divine energy, the divine expression. This movement reflects the entire truth about liberation. We should drop any fixed ideas we have about enlightenment, such as the illusory belief that it brings total goodness, bliss, and purity.

Life simply goes on. Occasionally, I may get angry, feel anxiety, or be in relationship with Claire. When the contraction passes, I quickly return to an all-encompassing acceptance in which the sense of separateness drops away, allowing us to live in love and see the same light. We live in that light, apparently together.

Questioner: *Is that the connection you both feel?*
Tony: To a large extent, the characteristics in my body/mind live with the characteristics in hers, and it works very well as a harmony in the world.

Questioner: *Without a sense of separation, how can independent experiences take place?*
Tony: It can because everything is the divine expression. Everything is the Absolute or the no-thing manifesting as creation, and you are the source of that. Whatever arises in that awareness is the beloved. Let's say that you have feelings, which you identify as your own. After awakening, you regard them as just feelings that apparently arise in "this," all of which is paradise. You could say that you walk around in your own paradise, and I walk around in mine. In this moment what's arising in my paradise is That. But "I am That" doesn't mean that I need to know what your paradise is like because once I'm in paradise, nothing more needs to be added.

Knowledge of your feelings won't add anymore to "my"

paradise because my paradise is always complete.

Questioner: *Why don't we experience everything as the whole?*
Tony: Your question implies that the mind has the capacity of being all-encompassing and all-knowing. For thousands of years, we've been taught that God is an omniscient, all-seeing being. This teaching comes from the male mind, which tries to keep everybody very small. When we really get it, we realize that being the all-knowing means no longer being separate.

We don't need to *know* anything. God doesn't know anything either because God is simply pure Being and love. Everything that arises in the body/mind is the pure Being of love, and no sort of knowing will ever add or detract from it.

Questioner: *So it's just a series of disjointed experiences?*
Tony: Except that they're all one experience of the divine. You talk about the universe, but who cares about that? What is the universe anyway? There are distant planets like Jupiter and Venus, but so what? What's above is what's below and completely one with the divine expression.

Questioner: *I understand that nothing more is needed, but something about the disjointed experiences makes them seem separate.*
Tony: That's how it seems to the mind, but really it's a mystery. Everything apparently arises in the one Source.

Questioner: *Is it one source with different experiences taking place?*
Tony: Don't forget that in the end nothing's actually happening. Again, it's a mystery. Nothing's happening, but

"this" simply arises. I don't think we can ever get to the bottom of it; the mind can never fathom this.

Remember, once awakening happens, questions about what appear to be separate experiences drop away.

Questioner: In this all-encompassing light and love, how would you answer the "why Hitler" question?
Tony: Hitler was only an appearance. Consciousness appeared in the form of Hitler and apparently carried out actions through him. There was no "Hitler" who had any choice at all. As just another appearance, it was the invitation in one of its innumerable forms.

Questioner: But why even talk about light and love as though there were something other than them?
Tony: Then you can call it "awareness," which is the source of all that is. Absolute awareness is the still, silent source from which everything emanates. From it everything comes forth in creation, including an apparent person called Hitler. Hitler arises in awareness, but so do Christ, Yehudi Menuhin, and Mother Teresa. It's all simply a richness that is arising as an invitation.

Questioner: And the mother who's repulsed by her daughter?
Tony: Yes, absolutely. It's all the divine expression.

Questioner: Maybe we'd be a lot better off without our minds.

Tony: When there's no one there, the mind is a great joy.

Conclusion

Let's close our eyes and be open to the possibility that there's no one there, that there's simply awareness—silent, still, impersonal awareness—and whatever seems to be happening is arising in that. Just be the watcher. As you watch what's arising, don't bring any judgment into what you perceive, whether they're noises, feelings in the body, or thoughts. Whatever there is, let it simply arise in nothing.

Let your questions fall away and stop trying to work anything out. Drop everything, including the person who's been sitting on your shoulder and passing judgment on your life. Let there be no boundaries, just space. Let the beloved arise in that space in whatever form it takes. You *are* the stillness; you *are* the silence in which everything arises. Embrace that which never moves and is totally still.

CHAPTER THREE

Encinitas

Day One

"Nothing exists that isn't
the invitation. You live in
total, constant
invitation."

I t's good to begin today by dropping any expectations about achieving or acquiring something. It's good to completely withdraw that person who wants things, who wants to get something. You can move away from any of those ideas and just sit in "this," which is the most valuable kind of sitting. I won't give you anything because you don't need anything. You are sitting in the midst of everything; you are everything. Perhaps some of you believe that you won't "get" it, but it's not "you" who are going to get it. When "you" are out of the way, then presence, which is always available, manifests as love and Being. That's what runs this whole manifestation—presence. There is only presence, there is only awareness, and body/minds carry that awareness, believing they are separate individuals. As a separate individual, we believe we need to "get" something or that something needs to happen—some sort of explosion—which will make things different. We believe that after this explosion, all feelings of frustration and fear will simply evaporate. That's not how it is. Fear, anger, and anything else that seems to happen in this apparent world can still arise in the body/mind.

Since I am everything that is, this includes the anger that arises in awareness. So enlightenment or awakening has nothing to do with dropping desire, the ego, or thinking, all of which take place within the background of awareness and unconditional love. "This," which is totally neutral, is liberation and it embraces everything. I embrace everything because I am everything that arises. There can't be any exclusion, nor can there be any denial. In awakening, there is no denial because everything is embraced by the lover.

You don't need anything from me because you *are* the lover, and whatever is happening in your body/mind for your body/mind is the beloved. You are always in invitation to see that you are the One, the light that allows this creation to be. There's nothing that can be done because there's no doer. Awakening is simply the realization that there is no separate individual. The illusion of the separate "me" drops away, and what remains is what already is: the one constant lover. What is taking place here is actually very ordinary and simple. There's no one to see or hear; there's just seeing or hearing. All the senses experience only the beloved's invitation. So let there just be seeing, hearing, and sitting on a seat. Let there be feelings of boredom, frustration, or misunderstanding, along with any other thoughts. Let all that be present, for it is all the beloved, all the invitation. Nothing exists that isn't the invitation. You live in total, constant invitation.

You can never escape from a tiger, and in the same way, you can never get away from the beloved. You can't escape what you are, which is the source of unconditional love. It's hard to convey this in words, but you are the Absolute, the source, the no-thing from which everything arises. And this includes the body/mind, that person you believe you are. The whole drama of this manifestation is the search to discover that there is no individual. There's still a Tony Parsons, you know. I am the light of all that is, but there are also the characteristics of Tony Parsons' personality, the sound of the voice, the feelings. All of this goes on, but it's not what I am. I am the light that allows all this to be. Once this is seen, a great adventure begins, whose nature is freedom. Then it expands. At first, one sees that "I am the awareness that arises," and then one embraces something else. When that something is integrated, one no longer identifies with anything at all, but with That, which is beyond words.

So Tony Parsons doesn't live in constant awareness or constant anything. Nothing happens anymore except ordinary life without question or judgment. We are not talking about detachment, but about a love affair. Simply sit back, don't expect anything, and the lover will appear. Otherwise, it's like walking through a jungle with a great big machete called meditation, hacking down all the leaves that are in the way in order to find a path to a destination. If you go on hacking at all the leaves with a great sense of endeavor and expectation, you'll become totally exhausted, drop to the ground, give up, and lie down. Just then a deer arrives and kisses your nose. It's very simple and immediate. It's all there is.

Questioner: *Tony, how can you sit there and say that you're the source of everything, that you're the light? In saying these things, aren't you just an imposter?*

Tony: You are the *I Am*, and so am I. The difficulty arises because if I say to you that you are the "source," the mind will usually imagine that it is an "individual" who is the source. That's the difficulty. Tony Parsons is not the light that allows this creation to be; he is part of that creation which arises, in the same way as the wall over there. Tony Parsons sits on a chair, speaking. If I say to people, "You are the source"—which I often do—it still can be misleading in one way or another. There's no one in this room except awareness, including the body/minds who believe they are people. There's only awareness here. You are the space in which awareness sits and allows creation to be.

Questioner: *Occasionally, I experience exactly what you're talking about. But I'm confused about how to live in the world. I feel compelled to do something to heal and alleviate the*

suffering I see. If I encountered people who were suffering and said to them, "How interesting—you're dying" or "Sorry that you're starving, but that's your reality. I'm going to have a cup of coffee, and I hope things get better. You know, it's just not real." I'd feel like a fake.

Tony: A certain body/mind is conditioned to respond to what it sees as suffering, and no one can do anything about it. Consciousness lives through that body/mind, expressing what you just shared with us. I'm suggesting that there is something that you can see that will not devalue how your body/mind responds to starvation or suffering. Life and the response to it still go on, but you're no longer identified with it, nor do you need to feel good or worthy to help people. When that goes out the window, there's a tremendous freedom in every action, and activities take place without any confusion about how to act anymore. Along with this, the habit of giving people an identity as "sufferers" also disappears. Suffering still takes place, but in the end you see clearly that "no one" actually suffers. Suffering just happens as an expression through particular body/minds. When you see this, you have much greater freedom in interacting with people because you're no longer adding the suffering aspect to their identity, which only exacerbates the whole idea of their suffering. In the end, drinking coffee on the beach in San Diego is just as sacred as putting tents up in Africa to alleviate suffering.

All this is only an appearance. It isn't leading to anything, and it never actually changes. Since this whole appearance is an external play based on the battle between good and evil, the world will always be in crisis. Will enlightenment save the world? It will always be a constant play that has absolutely no meaning at all. Your apparent life and this world have absolutely no meaning whatsoever except as an invitation. It's just an invitation to awaken and discover that you are the light, you are the Absolute, you are the energy, and you are the source of the manifestation. Once the invitation card is taken up—by no one—it ultimately turns into a celebration of creation. Then whatever arises for you, whether it's feeding the poor in Africa or not, no longer matters. The whole experience changes from being an obligation to a celebration. Freedom arises in letting go of the person called Tony Parsons, in my case, who drinks coffee on the beach in San Diego and who is not involved in saving the world.

The good works that we do and the efforts that we make to improve the world are only a reflection of the love that's beyond all this, a reflection of a love so radiant that there's no longer any compulsion to do anything in that light. As long as there's a sense of being a separate individual, all we can do is our best from that conditioned point of view. What I'm suggesting is that we see beyond that limited, judgmental view.

Questioner: *It seems to me that the place from which you speak encompasses more than just awareness, but love as well. Is this love separate from awareness? Is it some kind of energy? Does it obligate us to do anything?*

Tony: In the words of Nisargadatta Maharaj, while absolute wisdom sees that "I am nothing," absolute love sees that "I am everything." Everything is generated from unconditional love. All of creation is only unconditional love manifesting as a wall, a flower, or a candle. Here is unconditional love candle-ing; you are unconditional love Mary-ing or Joe-ing. All of this is generated from a fully liberated, unconditional love, beyond our ordinary concept of love, which tends to be narrow and possessive. Unconditional love is totally radiant; it fills everything, but it's neutral in the sense that it allows everything to be as it is. It's a liberated love, which allows any form of manifestation, including Hitler or whatever madman you can think of, to arise.

And awaking is certainly beyond just awareness. Some people teach that awakening is seeing that there is no "doer," that consciousness is all there is. But there's something that *knows* that consciousness is all there is. It is the lover, the ultimate, what you are. The idea of an "awareness being" is a kind of stuck-ness in which love has not yet blossomed.

Questioner: *You spoke earlier of everything being a manifestation of the divine expression, including the ego. But the ego veils our ability to see what's real. If we allow everything to be as it is, including the ego, won't it act as a veil that prevents us from seeing reality as it is?*

Tony: It depends what your idea of the ego is. If what you've described is your idea of the ego, then yes, it certainly falls away when awakening takes place because there is no longer a veil. But let's be clear: There's no longer a veil as far as seeing "I am That," but the ultimate awakening, based in absolute clarity, is not an individual thing, so this body/mind is still this body/mind. And the ego is then accepted, since it is seen as part of this manifestation.

Questioner: *Are you saying that by accepting the ego it can* *coexist with an awakened view of life?*

Tony: Anything can exist in oneness, which is beyond having a "view" of life.

Questioner: *I think I intellectually understand the impersonal aspect of enlightenment. But there's something still that believes that it's "me" that will be awakened. This is where the difficulty lies, isn't it?*

Tony: Can I share what goes on for Tony Parsons? In an ordinary day, I can simply say that anything can arise, even a sense of there being a character here who has a personality with a certain color and flavor that can be seemingly affected by what goes on outside. That personality is hardly the way that it was before the awakening, but nevertheless there's still an identity with someone called Tony Parsons. And if you call that ego, that's what I would call ego, too—the sense of a personality that's here, that walks around and moves, and that has certain characteristics. This goes on, but I simply see and accept that I am the opening for it to happen. I see it happen, it is accepted, and it is celebrated by no one.

Questioner: *In your first book,* As It Is, *you describe awakening while walking through a park in England. Could you elaborate*

on how you now see things differently?

Tony: The illusion of separation simply dropped away and there was oneness. Whatever attributes Tony Parsons has, whatever might occur with him, is simply what happens in the game of life. I am the love that allows all this to be. This love has nothing to do with Tony Parsons becoming less anxious or less greedy because it accepts everything, including greed or anger as part of the one manifestation.

Questioner: *Is this the maturity that you speak about? If anxiety or anger arises, do you see it for what it is, without denying it or pushing it away? Do you accept its reality at that moment but don't attach to it?*

Tony: Yes, except that I wouldn't use that phraseology because there's no individual who sees anxiety; there's just anxiety arising. It lives like this [snaps his fingers] and is gone like that simply because something else takes its place. It doesn't have anything to catch hold of because there aren't any hooks left. I don't identify with it, nor do I have any idea that it's wrong and should therefore change or improve myself. The feeling lives for a moment, is loved, and then it's gone. It's just a divine game.

Questioner: *I'll take a risk here and say that for most of us the ego still arises. If, as you say, there's no one to make an effort or achieve anything and nowhere to go by no one, how, then, does one lift the veil?*

Tony: You can't and you never will. You can't lift the veil because the veil is the idea of you.

Questioner: *How does one drop it, then?*

Tony: One doesn't drop it. It's dropped by *seeing* that there is no individual, but only space in which things apparently happen. You get a sense of moving "behind" the person that's always been in the forefront of things. Just behind that apparent person is the one that *knows* the person standing there looking at me. All of us here know that there's something just behind, watching us and looking at all this. Incidentally, what's happening here is that you're listening to yourself. It's "me" speaking to "me", and something within you knows it.

Questioner: *Is any sort of practice futile?*
Tony: Who's going to practice?

Questioner: *It seems to me that the opposite of practicing would be carrying on like everybody else. The majority of people in the world are just going about their way, taking the ego to be real.*
Tony: In a way, all people are searching. They're looking for something, whether it's wealth, power, or security, but what they're really looking for is "this." As a seeker, once you recognize that what you're looking for is beyond "you," you discover a readiness to die on the part of the one who's seeking. With this comes a tremendous relaxation. You can just stand the way you're standing and be the unique way you are because nothing has to change, and everything is absolutely, divinely appropriate. The way you are right now is exquisite. This is nothing more than a total change of perception, rather than self-improvement or change. Seeing what you are is totally exquisite, just as it is, with all the ideas, possible neurosis, and problems that the body/mind believes it has. This is its unique way to be.

Questioner: I appreciate what you're saying, but before you realized this, you were on some sort of a search, a quest to understand what this life is all about, which is different from what your average Joe is doing. Would you call this seeking a practice?

Tony: It's the final step that's taken. Most people live their lives without seeking enlightenment. At death, of course, they find what they've always sought all their lives because they've never moved away from it. Searching for the final resolution becomes the final seeking; it's all the same seeking. It's just that you've refined it down to the "final" search, which incidentally, of course, is the death of you, the realization that there is no "you."

Questioner: You speak about there being no change, but I've experienced a significant change in that I no longer identify with an angry "I" when there is anger. It's spontaneously released, and my next actions come from a completely different place. I also find healings within the body when I don't own it anymore and just allow it to be. So I'm a bit confused at this moment because I've had great changes take place in my life.

Tony: Every question has a unique answer, but what I'm basically saying is this: People don't have to look for a totally different way of living. If awakening happens, you don't rush to the nearest cave or become an enlightened master making a lot of money as I am. You can still go on being a car dealer or building contractor. Your way of life doesn't necessarily have to change, just your perception, which has happened in your case.

Questioner: *A whole range of emotions seems to arise in the body/mind. Is there an observer or witness of all this? I ask this because you use the word "watching," which sounds similar.*

Tony: As far as I'm concerned, observation is still an aspect of the mind. For me, self-observation, simply means that the mind is watching the mind. Self-observation has no relationship to awakening at all because with it there's usually a judgment or analysis of what's taking place and what needs to change. This has nothing to do with liberation.

Watching, however, takes place when one is open to seeing and discovering one's original nature. There does *seem* to be a watching, which is why I suggest to people that there's something behind them, watching them sitting and looking at me. This realization represents the first opening for many people.

Questioner: *Is this an all-inclusive type of watching?*

Tony: Yes, but that falls away, too, just as the invitation falls away in the end. Once the invitation is accepted, there's no need for it. The watching and the invitation are, in a way, preliminary steps that appear to be a process but really aren't. They seem to arise when there's an opening to the realization of our original nature. The beginning of awakening occurs by simply seeing what's arising.

Questioner: *In this beginning of awakening, as one's contentment deepens, does the personality's connection to* *emotions drop, or is there a deeper state in which they don't even arise?*

Tony: No, they do arise, but this has nothing to do with individuality. Emotions still arise in this body/mind, although they don't have the same dramatic urgency because there's no great charge to them anymore. An emotion simply arises, lives for a few seconds, then is no more. These emotions arise but have nothing to do with the individual; they are related to the whole of creation.

Questioner: *Can contractions arise as one deepens in this understanding?*

Tony: Yes, they can. But nothing can last for very long because there's no one to take delivery of it. I keep coming back to the fact that awakening has absolutely nothing to do with an individual—I am not "awakened"—and if somebody tells you he or she is awakened, walk away or just say, "Yeah, sure, and I'm Shakespeare." It's meaningless. Awakening takes place, but you'll never find an awakened person. I don't see anybody here; I see only Being in the form of apparent people.

Questioner: *Earlier you spoke about a watcher behind the head, a witness of all that goes on in our lives. My wife has had a similar experience. Can you say a bit more about the watcher?*

Tony: As far as Tony Parsons is concerned, there was a sense of "the watcher" before walking across the park. It suddenly appeared while I was busy doing things. It was totally impersonal, a bit frightening in a way, and a bit strange because of its impersonality.

Questioner: *Did it seem as if there were two of you?*
Tony: Yes, in a way, the watcher and me.

Questioner: *Both were in an equal balance?*
Tony: The watcher was far greater in me than any sense of myself. Don't forget, for me this whole thing began in Christianity, although I didn't last very long in the Christian tradition. Basically, there was a sense of God watching, but that soon fell away when I realized there was no such thing as God. When we awaken from the illusion of an external watcher, we discover an inner one, which is uniquely different for each person (certainly the way they describe the opening is different).

Some people seem to notice a great influx of what they call neurotic behavior once the "me" has dropped through awakening. For some people, this behavior may come out with guns blazing. Sometimes people phone me and say, "God, my worst fears are now taking place. What's happening?" Another thing that takes place after an awakening is what I call "the desert." It involves the total devaluing and dissolution of any ideas or concepts we have about our lives and their worth.

Let's be very clear about this: As far as I'm concerned, nobody here has a "life," and nobody's life is ever going to work. Yet we believe our life is going to work and we try to make it do so, but it never does. This leads to deep disappointment, which in turn leads to the invitation and love. So stay disappointed, and you will look somewhere else for happiness.

As people continue to hear this message, the mind goes on saying, "Yes, but . . . yes, but," and then it just gives up. For a while, though, they feel this sense of being in a desert as they begin losing the value they attached to their lives as they knew them. They actually lose hope because they realize that they're not going to get "better," and they can't make their lives go in a certain direction. For these people (again, not for everyone), it's a bit similar to Christ's time in the desert when the scaffolding of the old life falls away. The values they held are no longer relevant, nor have they anything to get excited about because they haven't yet fallen in love. When people phone me and complain, I tell them to just go on being intimate with "this," and soon the falling in love will happen. When all hope for a better life and a better "me" falls away, all that remains is "this," and really, there's always only this.

Questioner: *Falling in love with "what is" is a very delicate and extremely refined experience. I imagine that this is the next stage in our development because it opens us up. But what happens after that? I'm afraid that it could get very flat, arid, and desert-like.*

Tony: Not at all. We need to be careful because we're talking about awakening in a conceptual manner. While some people do get through a temporary desert-like period, what actually happens is the dropping of the sense of separation. Thereafter, of course, they see everything from another point of view. When people talk about this to me, I know it's genuinely happened because they can't really describe it. They often say, "It's amazing! This is so ordinary, yet it's so magnificent and absolutely stunning." They also say, "Why doesn't everybody get it? Why doesn't everybody see that it's the nearest thing to them right now? It's nearer than anything else, including their own breathing. It's simply Being and pure presence." After awakening there's a direct, immediate, and complete transformation. It doesn't happen to everyone, but it happens to many.

Questioner: *When awakening happens, there appears to be a shift in which ordinary consciousness allows the greater consciousness to take up residence. Is this correct?*
Tony: Let's go a little further with this because it's quite interesting. This is an amazing time to be alive because many people have a deep comprehension of awakening. I continually meet people who don't really need to hear very much because they already comprehend this. More and more people are ready to respond to this direct message in its absolute purity.

After awakening, people need to integrate what's happened to them. Very often they rush out and say, "I'm giving *satsang* on Friday," even though there's been no integration. For Tony Parsons, even some years after awakening, the idea persisted that there was still a need for greater unfoldment for this to mature. Some years later, there was a sudden seeing that there never was anyone and that awakening hadn't happened to anyone.

Although I experienced great clarity walking across the park, it took some time to integrate the vast seeing that, "This is all there is." Soon after the realization dawned that there's "no me" and that "there's nothing that can be done," speaking began to happen—with individuals at first and then more publicly. A lot of people start teaching, thinking that they can help others attain what they have, but if they haven't integrated their awakening, their teachings may create some confusion.

Questioner: I'm glad to hear this. For years I've been experiencing an arid awareness, dry and juiceless, yet profound, where name and form really don't exist. Although initially it seemed that this experience of awareness was extraordinary, it lost the quality of heart and affection.

Tony: It hasn't been lost, but something's moved away from you.

Questioner: It was instructive to hear your comments about neurosis. During the past few weeks, I have had horrendous bouts of obsessive thinking. If the mind wanted to reveal its insanity, it couldn't have done a better job. Realizing my divine identity somehow helps release ownership of all this neurosis. What you just said amounts to bringing the heart into this desert and being intimate with "what is."

Tony: One of the difficulties people have in approaching the beloved stems from what I call the "male approach." Even though I don't see "men" or "women" anymore, some body/minds may lean toward a more masculine approach, while others may lean toward a more feminine one, although they can appear equally in either sex. The difficulty with the masculine approach is that it tends to be somewhat dry, having a huge investment in the idea of awareness.

Somehow being "pure awareness" has a safe feeling about it. People feel safe in "being awareness" and letting things arise, without having to be engaged in anything anymore. They no longer have to be involved in any sort of intimacy and can remove themselves to the "glass box of awareness" where "things just arise." They take this to be the final liberation and feel free at last from having to be alive. To a certain extent, we are conditioned about suffering by traditional teachings, which come from the apparent male view of purity, abstinence, and detachment, all of which lead to dryness.

Questioner: *This certainly doesn't sound like fun.*
Tony: No, it isn't fun, but it's very attractive for those who want to stay safe. Awakening is actually a marriage of the masculine and feminine approaches. In its beautiful, exquisite clarity, awakening has a masculine feel about it. However, to be complete, it needs the earthiness of the feminine, with its love, deep intimacy, and groundedness. Without the feminine, awakening is only partial and needs to be married with its other half. When people tell me that they feel they're in an arid desert, I suggest that they become intimate with feeling the body, opening to it, becoming soft and malleable, and letting the sweetness of these sensations invade their "awareness." Eventually, of course, things balance out, and one approach is no longer stronger than the other.

Questioner: *Isn't this what Tantra teaches?*

Tony: Yes, in this respect Tantra was a primary religion. However, brilliant ideas generally become organized, turned into religions, and become dead. That's what happened to Tantra.

It's like the monk who went to work a monastery where they were making copies of the scriptures. His job was to write and translate them, but he noticed that the monks were simply duplicating copies from older copies; they weren't translating from the original texts. He thought there might be a mistake in the copies, so he asked the master if he could go down into the cave and look through the original texts.

So he did, and about two days later people noticed he was missing. They went to look downstairs and found the monk crying his eyes out. They asked, "What's the problem?" He said, "I've been carefully reading through the sacred texts, and I suddenly realized that the word is not 'celibate,' but 'celebrate'"!

The difficulty with Tantra is that the mind grabs hold of the idea that it can find God through sex, which then becomes another "way." We don't realize that we're always in sexual union; we're always in a state of intimacy with the beloved. This love never leaves us and is always reminding us of its presence by metaphorically tapping us on the shoulder. We're always in that love.

Questioner: *In some forms of Tibetan Tantra, love is the constant contact we have with the energy of life, and sex is nothing special because everything is based in the masculine and feminine.*

Tony: In a very ordinary way.

Questioner: *I believe that if we all lived in constant awareness of who we really are, there wouldn't be any violence or abuse.*

Tony: We're fascinated with the idea that we actually live a life and can influence events. This notion prevents us from realizing that "no one" has a life. Life is designed that way. Most people believe they're individuals and simply don't have any idea about what we're discussing. To them, this is madness. Actually, it's the complete opposite of the conditioned state they live in. The media goes on and on reinforcing that conditioned state, so naturally they'll always look at the awakened state as sheer madness.

Questioner: *If everybody knew about awakening, what would it mean?*

Tony: There isn't anybody to *know* anything. I don't know anything. But what you're suggesting is that all body/minds in the world would suddenly awaken.

Questioner: *Yes. What would happen then? Would we live the same way? Would life arise in the same manner that it arises now?*

Tony: The problem with this sort of thinking is that it's linear. It's based on the idea that there has been something happening for a few thousand years and that it's going to continue happening. It's not like that at all.

Questioner: *People generally look for truth and add it as a*

possession to whatever existing mental constructs they have.
They then "have" the truth and think that it will be really great
"for me." I realized that the truth will never serve anybody; all
it will do is wonderfully and utterly destroy you. I was reflecting
on the long spiritual journey that so many of us have been on
and how many of the traditions engage us within our
conditioning rather than outside it. Two years ago, I explored
Siddha Yoga, with its emphasis on shaktipat and the Siddha
Guru. I believed that I got shaktipat and experienced the
kundalini rising and thought, "Boy, this is really going to be
great for me."

Even though we were told to "honor, worship, and meditate
on our own Self," the power behind it was distinctly dualistic.
Clearly, there was a "you" who would achieve something in the
future, and then everything would be okay. Of course, other
traditions share this concept. It's so wonderful to have all of
this erased and to hold the perfection that is always present—
now.

Tony: It's just amazing how much conditioning we have about
the progressive path. The mind in its madness creates the idea
of a progressive path leading somewhere. These ideas are not
only present in the East, but also in Christianity, which teaches
that purification is necessary, that we have to change ourselves,
and that we can never be worthy enough. The traditions say
that there is a self that can be glorified or improved on.

What's interesting is that we live in an age of
understanding. We understand so many things about the
nature of this apparent creation, but what's growing alongside
this understanding is clarity. It's stunning that some people
are now communicating the truth in a very direct and simple
way. And others are ready to hear their messages. They're ready

to let their conditioned ideas go. It's really wonderful.

Questioner: *Tony, let me frame this question as the devil's advocate. How would you answer people who say, "What do we really know? Scientifically, ninety-five percent of the universe is unknown matter and unknown energy. Therefore, we can only imagine five percent of the truth."? From this point of view, someone might say, "You've had this experience, and it feels better than the way you were, but it's just a magnificent game that the mind is playing at a very sophisticated level to feel safe."*

Tony: This has nothing to do with being safe. It's the most dangerous place to be in because it's living in the unknown.

I was talking about our level of understanding of the universe. There's no question that everything takes place in manifestation, but only apparently. Alongside the created world is a greater, much clearer awareness of our original nature.

In some ways, the world we live in has always been mad, but in this apparent world, it appears that this madness is growing faster. However, alongside this madness is a reality that's completely neutral and completely, exquisitely balanced at all times. Of course, it looks dramatic, what with war in the Middle East and other hot spots. However, everything is in completely neutral balance. I watch the madness, yet it's balanced by "this," the stillness.

Questioner: *Tony, this is the first time I've met you or spoken with you. You talked about the different stages you've seen people go through after they experience a profound disillusionment with the mind, which leads to the desert. I have that feeling about my life right now, and it's not fun at all. In fact, it's pretty painful. My question is, "What's the next stage of development after that? Is it surrender to life or a letting go of identification?"*

Tony: There isn't anything that you can do about what happens next because there's no "you." When an opening takes place in the body/mind, then apparent stages of development seem to happen. These stages don't happen to everyone. For example, some people don't go through that desert. For them, awakening simply is there. For other people, there does seem to be a walk through the desert. After that, one of a million things can happen. There is no formula for this because there are no reference points.

A woman who came to one of the talks was near dropping her imaginary "self" and was trudging through the desert. What we imagine as the voice of the devil may come to such a person and say, "Look, you're in the desert now, so I can offer you realization." In this particular case, this woman was offered a technique to find enlightenment by someone living in America. She was so near awakening that it became frightening to her, and when she heard about this technique, she ran back to the idea of actually attaining something.

This is one such temptation and mirage that can happen in the desert. There are as many things that can happen as there are apparent body/minds in this creation, and each one is unique.

Questioner: *Yesterday, in speaking about meditation, you said that if it were done long enough, one would become bored. What do you mean by "bored"? Do you mean one that would cease trying for attainment, stop inquiring, or give up changing oneself? Should we just accept things as they happen and stop trying to do anything about it?*

Tony: Well, if you're trying to reach a certain state of being or behavior, you never will. You're actually making life conform to your ideas of how you could be. Just go on accepting life exactly as it is, which is meditation. Actually, there isn't anybody in the world who isn't meditating.

Questioner: *So I should accept life as it is?*

Tony: People try not to, but even their resistance is the divine expression. The resistance to life is the divine resisting life. Truly, there is no formula for awakening. Meditation or its lack will not bring about anything at all. Acceptance or nonacceptance of life will not bring about anything, either. Only the realization of your utter helplessness can bring about the understanding that "there's no one standing there." That's all that can happen. But you can't *do* this; no one can do it. No one can *do* anything.

Questioner: *I'm still a bit unclear. Is this an example of what* *you mean by becoming bored with meditation?*

Tony: Yes, it is giving up the idea that "this guy" can do anything.

Questioner: *So giving everything up just happens. Nobody does it, because it just apparently happens?*

Tony: Yes. As part of the invitation to see exactly who you are, you don't need to *do* anything. The way you stand, walk out of the room, and get into your car; the way you eat your lunch, the way you breathe and look at the sky: all these are it. Why do anything? You can sit in your kitchen with a cup of coffee and think, "I'll go upstairs to my sacred altar, light the candles, and meditate." But why the hell do anything special when the kitchen table and the cup of coffee are sacred? God is expressing as the table and cup of coffee.

Questioner: *I don't know how to express this. The apparent giving up and the apparent absence of striving and trying to figure things out are just what is. How do these different aspects of life balance each other?*

Tony: The world as it appears is in total balance because it's completely neutral. It isn't good nor is it bad. It's how unconditional love, which is totally neutral, appears. Unconditional love presents an apparent world to apparent people, who think that life is a great series of happenings that has meaning and that leads them somewhere. That's the joke: the belief that our lives have meaning and everything that happens to us is a lesson or a teaching from God. We say, "God has done this to teach me such and such," when in fact life is just a meaningless appearance that is perfectly balanced.

Questioner: *You said earlier that the dark side of life—the wars and madness that we see on television—is balanced by more people in the world waking up.*

Tony: That's right. There is a balance of negative and positive energy in the world.

Questioner: *How does that work?*

Tony: You tell me. You did it! It's an exquisite work of genius, the most incredible happening there is. But in truth, nobody did it; it's the manifestation of unconditional love.

Questioner: *I was awakened last night at eleven o'clock by a family member who was in jail because of a drug problem. What a disappointment. Of course, life is full of such things. I took a long walk and allowed the disappointment to be there without doing anything about it. I realized that part of me feels that drugs and alcohol are a hindrance to awakening and that I still have judgments about this.*

Tony: So there's someone there who has a judgment.

Questioner: *I guess there still is.*

Tony: It's difficult with judgments because they're conceptual. But they also contain a sense of emotion, a feeling in the body that's related to what arises out of the judgment about drugs. Do you sense a feeling arising?

Questioner: *Yes, but it just distorts things.*

Tony: But the feeling is the beloved. The story about drugs is just a story. The information that: "Drugs do this and that" is the recording that plays in your mind. But the feeling in your body is the beloved. As you become intimate with the beloved, it's possible that suddenly there will be no one there except the beloved.

The member of your family in jail is uniquely a gift. Everything that occurs to us is a gift, and although the mind would like to judge his imprisonment as a bad thing, actually it's the beloved knocking on the door.

Questioner: Looking back at the values and beliefs I've lived with, I'm trying to figure out why I experience love with some people and not others. I assume it has something to do with my conditioning, beliefs, and upbringing. Could you speak more about our relationships and explain why we are open with some while closed with others, sometimes even unable to maintain eye contact?

Tony: When we're young and we fall in love with someone, it's usually a knock-out affair. Falling in love is something like enlightenment in that the sense of "me" temporarily falls away in the adoration of our partner. But awakening involves completely dropping any sense of "me" and falling in love with everything, including oneself. When this takes place, we simply love and accept everything.

We can still dislike someone because all that's left is actually a game. We all have particular game-playing tactics that we use to deal with life. And when we meet somebody and his game doesn't fit with ours, dislike arises. I don't like certain people. I may love what a person is, but I don't necessary like him. Not liking people just arises. There's nothing to do about it, and there's nothing wrong with it. In fact, there is nothing wrong with anything. Sometimes the chemistry doesn't work with certain people, so I don't want to be with them.

The difficulty arises because we have the idea that after awakening we simply love all things. This is pure nonsense. One of the characteristics that make up Tony Parsons may be disliking the sight of someone, but loving the source of the energy that he is. Again, there's nothing that I can do about it anyway.

Questioner: *I volunteer for a Suicide Prevention Hotline. When somebody calls, I first have to determine whether the person is serious about wanting to kill himself. After a rapport has been established, we talk about the resources that are available to the caller. By the end of the call, it's all so sweet. Although I've received professional training, I'm essentially on the line for the love, which often is so thick that you could cut it with a knife. I believe in self-determination, but we've been discussing the illusion of the separate self. How does service fit into the big picture? Am I really doing a service, or am I just meeting people where they are and dealing with them at that level?*

Tony: Actually, meeting people where they are and dealing with them at that level is the best of all because there's really no one whom you can serve; you can only be what you are. You are only responding to "what is." There's no one "here" serving anyone "there." There's no one "in here" who can serve because there's no one "out there" to serve. The idea of service is a form of colossal arrogance, expressed as "I will help you."

Questioner: I love this work so much. But while it seems futile to speak about these concepts with people, they do slip out every once in a while.

Tony: You don't help them when this happens. In a way, there's almost a "final phase system" that doesn't allow this sort of message to be communicated indiscriminately. It wouldn't be appropriate for people to hear it without a sense of readiness.

We naturally respond to people when they ask for help. What you're doing is setting up a way to help others. But when you open to awakening, you realize that there's no one to help. Helping then takes place as a natural response, which gives others a tremendous freedom to open up. If you go on randomly helping people, they may feel overwhelmed, convinced that they actually do need help. It's like a big circle.

Questioner: Yes, and it feels heavy. By the end of the call, it's as if we're both cured.

Another question: A number of young people call who are being abused in their homes. They want to end it, but they don't know any other kind of life. I've felt very lacking in my responses. I tell them, "You can't know what's ahead, so refrain from making a decision now." I don't know that my response is very positive.

Tony: No, but at least your answer has clarity. It opens up the possibility for something unknown to happen, which you don't have to anticipate. But I think that no matter what we're conditioned to believe about suicide or death, there's nothing terribly significant about either one. Western society invests a huge amount of energy in trying to preserve life and to prevent death or suicide. But neither is very significant at all.

Also, don't lose sight of the ordinary or get locked into emotional concepts, such as "life" and "death," because when we're gripped by them, we tend to overlook the beloved in the midst of the ordinary. The Kingdom of Heaven is like a mustard seed—it's in the tiniest of things.

Questioner: I've been a Buddhist for eight years. Recently, a man looked into my eyes, and I instantly was transported into a state of being that really freaked me out. I'm here today because I've fallen off the deep end, and it feels like I'm losing my mind. Yet, I feel excited and exhilarated at the same time. I see myself pulling away from my normal belief system. I wonder if you could expand on this.

Tony: Well, yes, in a way there's excitement, but not the kind one would normally associate with everyday life. It's not traumatic and exciting after awakening. Everything is more serene; the mountains are flattened and the valleys are raised. In a way, everything becomes more even. And in this integrated perception, one sees that, "I am Being, from which everything arises." One simply carries this perception around, embodying it in everything that appears. It's very ordinary; it's not at all dramatic.

Questioner: *But in my case, I make it dramatic.*

Tony: Yes, you do. Some people always look for dramatic experiences. The difficulty is that there are no dramatic experiences. There is no one there to have a dramatic experience. Whenever there is someone seeking, it reinforces the person who needs dramatic experiences.

Questioner: *I still want to hold on to my belief systems. It's so hard to . . .*

Tony: Do you have belief systems?

Questioner: *Yes.*

Tony: When you looked in the eyes of the man who looked into your eyes, didn't you awaken?

Questioner: *Yes, I did.*

Tony: Then why do you have any belief systems left?

Questioner: *I didn't have any in that moment.*

Tony: Then it was only for a moment?

Questioner: *Well, I've had many moments.*

Tony: I'm very suspicious about this "looking in the eyes" stuff. A woman who comes to my meetings in London once said, "You're too kind," and when she looked into my eyes, everything disappeared. So I said, "What are you doing here?"

Questioner: *You say that the experience of awakening is ordinary and very simple, but the understanding of it seems complex. It takes great intellectual ability to deconstruct all of this.*

Tony: No, not at all. Awakening is about childlike openness and simplicity. With understanding, you drop the concepts that your mind holds. Once understanding arises, all the ideas you've had about awakening just fall away. There's nothing very intellectual or complicated about it.

Questioner: *Perhaps I have a cultural problem. I'm from Brazil, a Third-World country. What really strikes me is how many white people are here. I've been in America for five years, and this is the first time I've experienced America in such a Caucasian way. As a Christian in Brazil, I went to a church where the poor and rich, the educated and uneducated, mingled together. In the city, slums are often located right next to the homes of rich people. Do you feel that your message can be felt and embraced by people of all social, economic, and educational backgrounds? I raise this question because in America I see the message appealing mainly to the upper class. Have you had experience with people who come from other backgrounds?*

Tony: A gardener in London, an utterly simple man who used to study with me, is now doing his own teaching. He comes from a working class family and is not an intellectual in any way. At one time he did a lot of searching and conceptualizing, but in the end he came back to a natural way of being, which is simple, childlike, and full of wonder.

This message is for everyone. It's utterly simple, fully immediate, and totally here. For an intellectual person who clings to conceptual understanding, it may take time for it to fall away. In truth, though, we don't need to have any concepts about it at all.

Questioner: *When you say that awakening requires readiness, what is this readiness like?*

Tony: It certainly has to do with the longing to drop all knowing. There really isn't anything that you can do about readiness; it will either be there or it won't.

Questioner: *When you speak about self-hatred and self-love, I know that they are reflections of the outside in our inner experience. How do we allow for neurosis to come up? Are we just to be present with it?*

Tony: Yes, except that there isn't anybody *doing* it. There isn't anybody here allowing a neurosis to arise and to be accepted. Because there isn't anyone here but awareness, anything can arise in it, including neurosis. It simply arises in the "no-thing" that I am. Everything arises in this "no-thing," including Tony Parsons' or Tim's neurosis. But for Tim or anyone else, there's no outside or inside; there's only what is. There's no such thing as truth, but only what is!

Questioner: *How can you characterize the awakened state as* *being ordinary when it seems rather extraordinary to me? How can you characterize it at all?*

Tony: Can we just stay there for a moment? It's our natural state and our natural way of being. When awakening happens, we suddenly realize that we've come back home to how we naturally are, which is actually quite ordinary. It's wonderful to experience the magnificence of the ordinary.

Questioner: *It's the ordinary within the extraordinary . . .*
Tony: I don't like anything that is extraordinary, precious, or exclusive.

Questioner: *Why don't you like that?*
Tony: Because I have a passion about "this" and about this exquisite, useful, wonderful message, which is so ordinary. And I also have a great sword that will cut off the head of anyone who makes "what is" into something extraordinary and then gives it other people in its exclusivity. I want to chop of the heads of all those people who go around touting this message with an aura of holiness that excludes other people. Some teachers make a show of how they are to be presented. They dress specially, and their behavior separates them from others. Their message is "I'm special and you aren't."

Questioner: *In the realm of the ordinary, if something extraordinary happened, wouldn't it surprise you?*
Tony: No.

Questioner: *So you're not a good judge of what is ordinary.*
Tony: Oh, that's better. What is ordinary *is* extraordinary.

How can I communicate this? There is no way it can be

communicated, yet it is the most wonderful gift there is. Nothing else is worthy of this; nothing else even comes close to it. And so my passion is to express the inexpressible. I expressed this passion in my book, *As It Is*. I tried to write a book that was simple, to the point, and clearly written. What I find most wonderful is what's happening here—talking to people and communicating in this way. So much more happens in this environment than in any book you've read.

There are so many books written by great teachers that you can take home and read. A fragrance emanates from the words of such teachers as Ramana Maharshi, who remained mostly silent, but the most powerful thing is to sit with blood and bones—with nothingness. That's what's wonderful and what I'm passionate about. I'm also passionate about your seeing that the person speaking is an ordinary person, just like you. If there's nothing extraordinary about him, then like him, you, too, can say, "I am That." If I could, I would give up my life that you could see this. Really! Well, I *have* given up my life, so it's about time that you saw it.

Tony: This is one of my favorite stories that deals with religious concepts and tolerance:

A Hindu, a rabbi, and a Catholic priest were walking in the woods. Suddenly there was a heavy storm, so they ran to a nearby farm for shelter. They asked the farmer, "Can you put us up for the night because of this foul weather?" The farmer answered, "Yes, but I can only take two of you inside. One of you will have to sleep in the stable."

The Hindu said, "That's okay, I'll go out there and you two be comfortable indoors." After several minutes there was a knock on the door. It was the Hindu, who said, "There's a cow in the stable, which is sacred to Hindu tradition, so I must give the animal its space. May I sleep inside?"

The rabbi said, "That's okay, I'll stay in the stable." So the rabbi went out, and after a short while there was a knock on the door. "I can't stay in the stable," said the rabbi, "There's a pig in there. I just can't sleep with a pig."

So the Catholic priest said, "That's all right, I'll sacrifice myself and sleep in the stable so that you two can be comfortable inside." Soon after the priest left, there was a knock on the door. It was the pig and the cow.

Somebody was speaking earlier today about the confusion we have with our seemingly separate experiences. We appear to be our body/minds and our experiences. You can't experience what I seem to experience, so we appear to be separate. In this way, the dream of separation is reinforced. Why would Tony Parsons scratch his hand? I can't know what "that" is. But strangely enough, the experience I have is the same as the experience you have of scratching your hand in that it's all the beloved. These experiences arise in the beloved as simply pure Being. It just so happens that your experience has a different color than mine, so the events appear to be separate. Actually, it's all one Being.

Questioner: *So there's no itch; you're just scratching? I can't see the itch.*

Tony: No, and it doesn't matter because whatever arises—this scratching or your sitting on that seat—is all one thing, pure "is-ness." The ground of Being simply arises in different forms, which appear to apparently separate people as different experiences. There is nothing different; there is no separation between anything. One energy appears as everything in this multifaceted existence.

Questioner: *So I'm not experiencing itching, and there is no itching?*
Tony: You're not experiencing anything. "No one" experiences anything. What's really happening is that Being is manifesting in different forms. No one actually experiences this; one merely *appears* to experience it.

Questioner: *If someone has a terminal disease and is suffering with extreme pain, that's not the same as an "itch"?*
Tony: Yes, it is. Everything is Being manifesting in what appears to be differing forms: cancer, an itch, hunger, or anything else.

Questioner: *On the absolute level, it may all be one, but on a practical level, some of us who are in good health are thankful as opposed to someone who, unfortunately, has a life-threatening illness.*
Tony: Yes, as long as you feel that you're a separate individual, you'll compare one thing with another. Awakening ends such comparisons. One realizes that it's not best to be one thing or another, but only "what is."

Questioner: *But for most of us . . .*

Tony: Yes, for most people who believe that they're people, the hypnotic dream goes on, with the illusion of having a separate existence. Actually, that isn't really what's happening at all.

Questioner: Tony, if this feeling of separateness is in the mind, then the mind will have to give itself up. When we were talking over lunch, you said the mind has nothing to do with the present; it has no interest in the present. Afterward, I realized that the mind itself is time.

Tony: It's all used by consciousness. One thought creates the illusion of space and time, along with the past and the future.

Questioner: How does the mind, which has no appreciation of presence or openness, give up?

Tony: It simply stops seeking.

Questioner: By itself?

Tony: Well, yes, but it can't choose to do it. What apparently happens is that it stops looking. The realization dawns that there is no mind "in here" looking.

Questioner: It's like a painting of a man scratching his hand and an observer standing near a microphone. How can the observer record the apparent scratching sound that comes from the painting?

Tony: Yes, absolutely! This is a bit of a leap, but all of existence is actually one picture, one image. However, the mind believes manifestation is made up of different images that together tell the story. Actually, there is only one image, which is pure Being manifesting as "this," appearing to be a story. It's a joke, yet the comedian has an audience that never laughs at it!

You began all this before time emerged. As pure Being, you made the decision to change from being one by becoming two. You chose to play this game of apparent manifestation, with its apparent story and different experiences. In this game of separation, you pretend to be separate in order to return to the oneness. You decided to play the game. However, before you started to play, you also decided that everything in manifestation would be an invitation to go back home, to discover that you were playing a game called separation and that you are the one who started it.

Questioner: *But how do you know that?*
Tony: I *am* that.

Questioner: *Is this your experience both during and after the game?*
Tony: Yes. That's how it always is. You are always the presence of God pretending to be a separate person and discovering that you *are* God. And everything in existence is inviting you to see "you are That." You haven't vanished yet?

Questioner: *Not yet.*

Questioner: *Can one differentiate between consciousness and awareness?*

Tony: Yes. While it's hard to put this into words, we can point out that absolute awareness, Being, unconditional love, and the beloved are all "one thing." They are the singular no-thing from which everything emanates. So coming back to your question, we can say that awareness is the source of all that is. You *are* absolute awareness, and without absolute awareness, nothing can be. Consciousness is all that appears to arise. So you are the source of all that seems to be happening, including the illusion of separation and the longing to come home. Everything is part of consciousness arising as creation.

Questioner: *Why does the dream seem so incredibly real? We can observe that thoughts arise without there being a thinker as their source, yet our thoughts appear so real to us. Why is that?*

Tony: Well, I would say that it's a work of genius based on the energy that comes from unconditional love. The one creates the many, and in that plurality resides the whole illusion of separation that we play as a game. Illusion and separation manifest in an amazing way. Out of pure love creation arises as what's apparently "not love," so that we may appreciate love and return to it as the one falling in love with itself again.

Questioner: *When we talk about the One arising as the many, about unity becoming multiplicity, it really only happens in the moment, doesn't it?*

Tony: Yes, but I don't like the idea of moments because it implies some sort of continuity in time: There's this moment, and then there's another moment. But certainly the whole story of creation and destruction is happening as this, since it's always "this."

Questioner: As women, we've been conditioned to serve, so when you said, "Serve," it felt arrogant to me. It hit me hard because I felt the arrogance inside of me and it's ugly. You were saying how you like to chop heads off. Would you chop mine off?

Tony: I can't do that.

Questioner: Could you help me?

Tony: No. There's no way I can. You don't need any help; you can't be helped because you are That. No one else can make that happen for you.

Questioner: So the arrogance will continue to exist in some form?

Tony: I can't help you drop your idea of being mad at me. There is no one here anyway, so how can I help you? What happens is that concepts drop away and clarity takes its place. But something else also takes place that is so much more majestic. I can only describe it as an energy.

Questioner: So the arrogance has to be here until it ceases by itself, and then it flies into the beloved. Is there no judgment about it?

Tony: No. There's no way anything can be judged. There isn't anything to be judged. Everything is absolutely perfect as it is.

Questioner: You've said that it's not necessary to meditate. On the other hand, some people have meditated deeply and have become enlightened.

Tony: Do you know someone?

Questioner: The Buddha, although I don't know him personally.

Tony: Have you met him? Ask him if that's what happened.

Questioner: From my practice, it takes one to know one.

Tony: I don't know much about Buddhism, but my understanding was that he just gave up, and the flowering happened.

Questioner: He was practicing for a long time—for years.

Tony: He may have mediated for a long time, but it had nothing to do with him because there wasn't anyone there. Meditation apparently happened, but he ultimately gave it up and saw "I am That."

Questioner: Meditation practice reveals that there is "no self." You're saying the same thing.

Tony: No, I am saying that presence becomes apparent when giving up looking for it happens . . . but no one makes that happen.

Questioner: *Perhaps, for some people, but when you are an ordinary mortal like me . . .*
Tony: You're not an ordinary mortal.

Questioner: *I believe that murder is immoral and that we should do acts of charity like Mother Teresa. But apparent good and evil are both the same thing, and everything is in balance.*
Tony: Are you ready to move beyond those concepts?

Questioner: *Yes, I'm ready to be open to anything. Even though we're already That, can you suggest a practice to help us realize it?*
Tony: Practice is for someone who thinks he or she is an individual. What would be the purpose of the practice?

Questioner: *To be free.*
Tony: How can the self, which is not there, practice "being there," so it can find that there is such a thing called freedom?

Questioner: *But we still have to practice. In other words, if you want to take the bus, learn to read, or accomplish something, you have to "do" something. For example, I had to "do" something in order to get here.*
Tony: Yes, you apparently had to. If you want to run a mile in less than four minutes, you'd have to practice. If you want to attain anything, you'd have to practice. The one thing that you can never attain is your original nature. You'll never find or get that. We always think that doing this or that will help us get it, but it'll never happen.

As long as your mind holds the idea of achieving something, then traditional practice will take place, based on what you've learned about awakening. Without knowing that you are divine, you'll continue looking elsewhere for it.

Questioner: *But I know that we are all divine.*
Tony: No, you don't know it. You believe that you are Bill who is trying to find something. Be ready to be adventurous; be ready to chop all the heads off that are looking at you and telling you how you should be. Be ready to drop all of it.

All the traditions talk about freedom, but "this" is the freedom, not something written on paper. Forget the Buddha and chop his head off.

Questioner: *As the saying goes, "If you find Buddha on the road, kill him."*
Tony: Absolutely. And the Buddha tells you that you need to meditate, to practice right-mindedness and wise action. Chop off his head and rest in the arms of the beloved!

Questioner: *But that's so difficult because I don't know where I'll be going.*
Tony: You never will. Give up "knowing where you're going." If you want to be safe, you're in the wrong place.

Questioner: *Then how can I find safety?*
Tony: There's only one constant, safe place, and that's in the arms of the beloved where you're always safe and always held. It doesn't matter what happens to you in the life you think you're leading. You're actually always held in the divine arms. You can never leave the beloved because you *are* the beloved. Let go of trying to "know" it and just relax into what is.

Questioner: *You say that this is a perfect world in perfect balance. With the problems in the Middle East, we get the idea that the balance is going "off balance." And if you are living in Israel, then you really believe it.*

Tony: I think if you are living anywhere, you live in fear. Once there is a sense of separation, you live in what seems to be an alien world. There is no one who isn't afraid.

Questioner: *I stand here in this space and I see you; I look out here and see all the others. I wonder if you could share the experience that allows you to look out and not see the others?*

Tony: No, I can't do that.

Questioner: *I recently had an experience in the presence of a well-known American teacher in which there was just "it"— the lover and the beloved. I experienced a sense of oneness that I recognize as my original nature, who I really am. Now I miss and long for it. I know there's nothing that the mind can do to recapture it, except maybe surrender to it, but I really don't know how to surrender.*

Tony: You can't. Because the experience was so intense at the time, you long for it some time afterward. For some people this longing goes on for years. Of course, this longing creates another veil that pushes away the wonder of what is already here.

This very moment is presenting to you the immediacy of the beloved. This presence gets lost when you long to return to something that seemed to happen before. It can be like a curse, really.

Questioner: *I know. It was such a wonderful experience, yet it was just a glimpse.*

Tony: It's a glimpse of your original nature. Why don't you go and live with this person?

Questioner: *She's married.*

Tony: In a way, the mind says, "I should spend the rest of the year with this person and go on re-experiencing the sense of oneness." It won't happen, but the mind convinces us that it will.

Questioner: *I went on a silent retreat several months ago and found it very challenging to observe my mind. I saw how it pushes people away or wants to get something from them. I realized that's not how I want to be with people; I want to be with them heart to heart. I felt that this actually did happen.*

Tony: Yes, but you're describing being someone having a "heart-to-heart" relationship with other people. This has nothing to do with awakening. It's just another way of making the prison more comfortable. You may have glimpsed something that's slightly beyond the concept of being more open with people. I suggest that you drop the memory of that experience and all hopes of regaining it, and come to the wonder of pure presence. That glimpse gave you a foretaste of it. But there's nothing you can do to "get it" because there's no "me" who can do anything.

Questioner: *Then I should give that experience up, too?*
Tony: Oh, yes. Absolutely.

Questioner: *Actually, it's happened several times to me, which makes me believe that I'm on the trail.*
Tony: You can't say what you're on the trail to, but what you're looking for isn't really related to your first experience. When Tony Parsons walked across the park, a great light came into the apparent darkness in a way that was completely fascinating. Because it had never happened before, it was astounding. But it also never happened again because the light had dissipated the darkness. So because there was light, there was no contrast. That's what you want to experience, too. Forget the initial event; don't ever look for it again because it's never going to happen. It doesn't need to happen. The light has entered the darkness, and after that it becomes much more ordinary. It's all right for it to be ordinary.

Questioner: *I like the extraordinary.*
Tony: I know. Don't we all? This is one of the biggest difficulties for most people, who always look for the extraordinary.

Questioner: *But there are other times when I actually feel a connection with all of life, and it seems very ordinary.*
Tony: An opening is happening here, and I hope you see it when you walk back to your seat and leave this meeting. In a very real way, you will still be on retreat. Learn to be intimate with ordinary activities like peeling potatoes in the kitchen or

taking a shower. Close your eyes and vanish into the shower, and when you're cleaning your teeth, vanish into that activity. The ordinary is so peaceful, sweet, and beautiful.

Questioner: *In moments of deep listening, I've had a fleeting glimpse of the origin of this form.*
Tony: Of this form? Of this manifestation? It has no origin.

Questioner: *I've read that what's born arises from the unborn. I'm trying to find out more about the unborn mystery.*
Tony: In one way, there's no beginning, no origin. But in another way, the origin of everything is presence, Being. It isn't the origin of time, but rather the origin of manifestation.

Questioner: *Is it similar to waking up from the dreams that we have at night?*
Tony: There's a period in sleep when obviously there's no one. At that time we're home. But there's also a period of dreaming, which is actually a different form of dreaming, another manifestation of the mind. And it's a very clever dream because when you wake up, you think you've stopped dreaming. What you're really doing is dreaming in another form. It's another part of this brilliant work of genius.

Questioner: *So do we go from one dream to another dream?*
Tony: Yes. Our waking dream is a dream of separation.

CHAPTER FOUR

Encinitas

Day Two

"You never will get it
because you *are* it, just
the way you are."

Nothing needs to happen today. There isn't anything that's going to happen because it is already the case. You already are that which is sought, so you can go home now!

Dropping the seeker is awakening. Awakening, like the sun, is always shining. When clouds evaporate, what remains is the sun whose light is always shining. Everything that we see— the walls, apparent people, floors, flowers, and everything else—is simply light celebrating as manifestation and enjoying the game of separation. Consciousness enjoys the game of separation, which is maintained by beliefs, such as, "I'm not the light," "I don't get it," and "I'm a long way from it, and I have to work hard and become pure to find it because only very few ever attain it." God, who loves not knowing himself, so he can find himself again, is playing a game of hide and seek. One constant runs through this game: the light, the Being. It's hard to put this into words, but the manifestation is filled with presence, which is unconditional love. We use different words to point out the one thing, which is nameless.

No-thing is the constant from which everything emanates, and you are the no-thing. I don't mean you as Bill, Mary, or Henry, but you as the no-thing from which everything emerges. As part of the drama of manifestation, we believe that we're just a little individual searching for our original, timeless nature. While we enjoy the game of seeking, strangely enough, what we're looking for is the closest thing to us, even closer than our breath.

Presence, which is constantly with us, is very subtle, still, and silent. It exists behind thoughts, such as "I don't get what he's talking about" or "I'm still an individual looking." It remains the witness of our thoughts and feelings. It's always been there, watching everything that's gone on in our apparent life. Everything that's happened has been perfectly appropriate as an invitation to see behind all the activity into our true nature. Behind all the activity, searching, fighting, and struggling is the lover, who simply watches the game and waits for the activity to stop.

The lover watches the mind as it thinks, "To awaken I have to be pure, clear my chakras, forgive my mother, and meditate at least two or three hours a day." The lover watches all of our efforts, which are so endearing because they're so wonderfully ridiculous. We walk up the stairs to our meditation room, thinking that's where the miracle will happen, while we overlook that walking up the stairs is miraculous in itself. In truth, the divine is everywhere. The divine is smoking pot, drinking whiskey, playing tennis, or driving a car; everything is the divine expression. Everyone in this apparent world is living in the invitation to awaken and discover that there is no one. There is no such thing as an individual; there is simply Being pretending to be you and me. We can't do anything to awaken because there's no one to do it. No one can tell you to do anything or can help you do anything because nobody needs any help to awaken from the game of the one being two.

Imagine our investment in struggling to awaken and then suddenly realizing that there's no one here but only Being itself and "I am That," which allows everything to be. It can be agonizing to suddenly realize that everybody else is That, and you are unable to shake them into seeing the truth. Yet you don't need to convince everybody because everything is perfect as it is. You only have to drop the belief that you don't get it. You never will get it because you *are* it, just the way you are. All the funny things that you think aren't quite right are absolutely the divine expression. Nothing ever needs to change. Existence is singing the perfect song of love, inviting you to accept everything just as it is. When you see this, you will love and accept your body/mind—the person you think you live with—as well as everyone else. No longer does anything have to be better than it is, because in that radiance you accept everything just as it is.

Nothing ever happens; this whole creation is simply an appearance. It has absolutely no meaning. It'll never get better, and it'll never get worse. It's always like this. And the only purpose you'll find for creation is the invitation for the truth-seeker to awaken and rediscover that there is only one. Thereafter, the invitation turns to celebration. Nothing is going anywhere, and no one needs to go anywhere since this is it.

Does anyone want to ask anything?

Questioner: I was struck when you said that everything can only be as it is because there's nobody to make any decisions or choose anything different. It occurred to me that when we see this clearly, there's a simplifying in the body/mind, and any thought or resistance to "what is" becomes ridiculous. Can you confirm in your experience that the mind becomes simpler?

Tony: Oh, yes, because this is a totally revolutionary yet fundamentally natural way of seeing reality. We are conditioned to believe that somehow "I'm not quite right," "The world isn't quite right," and "We've got to do something about changing all of that." According to this conditioning, everything has to change for the better, including me.

It's revolutionary to see that actually nothing's happening at all, nothing has ever changed, and it's all the same thing painted in different colors. There's nowhere to go and nothing to do because there's no one who *can* go anywhere and because *this* is paradise. This revolutionary realization, which is beyond time and space, embraces them both totally. With this incredibly simple understanding, everything falls away, including all the concepts we have about how we should be and what enlightenment is.

Questioner: After awakening we can see clearly that all the mind stuff isn't us. When anger arises, an awakened person sees that there's no one there to be angry, and it falls away because there's no identifying with it. In your experience, is there something in the mind that resists what is? Does it dissipate with time and become less active?

Tony: Yes, it does, in what seems like time. Everything becomes more harmonious, and everything slows down. All the anxiety, angst, and the mind's positive and negative energies flatten out. As Christ said, "I will level the mountains and raise the valleys." When awakening happens, all the extremes are reduced. Anger can arise but can't live in that light. There is no one who hooks into it any longer, or no one has any interest in it, so it can't survive in that kind of light.

Questioner: *It strikes me that life is nothing but pushing and resisting. Although this happens in manifestation, what truly is has no resistance to the whole. It seems strange that out of this absolute nonresistance, neutrality, and love that this manifestation is pushing and resisting life.*

Tony: It appears to be, yes. But life emerges from unconditional love, which is utterly neutral, while the manifestation seems to have negative and positive energies that are in conflict all the time. They're always in a state of balance.

Questioner: *You've alluded to the fact that there's no such thing as space. Could you talk about that a little bit?*

Tony: Just as time is a concept, a thought form, so is space. Space is simply a representation of silence or stillness. In reality, no space exists between seemingly separate objects since both arise in stillness and are one with it. If we think of the past or anticipate the future, we think of it in consciousness. And in three years' time, we will still anticipate the future in some way. At all times, consciousness is all there is, appearing in the drama of time to make us search for that which lies beyond it but there's only "this."

Eventually, one sees that nothing's happening and that nothing has ever happened; things only appear to have happened. I'm not going to say, "All there is, is now." There's no "now" because now implies "then." There's no "moment," either. What I'm saying has nothing to do with living in the moment because there's no one to live it and no moment to inhabit. There's only "this" in which time appears to have intervened. Reality radiates this manifestation as pure Being. Although life appears to be composed of separate events, it's actually one photograph. The mind pieces together one apparently separate photograph with the next one and the next one, and it thinks that all these pictures tell a story. But it's simply Being that's manifesting, whose only meaning is the invitation to awaken.

In these kinds of meetings, several things can take place. People come together with concepts about who they are and what enlightenment is. It's possible that those concepts will be completely destroyed and that one will be left with absolutely nothing. In being left with absolutely nothing, without any expectation, one may suddenly see "this," the timeless wonder of Being.

The seeker is always denying God, liberation, and Being itself because he or she is always looking elsewhere for what is already present. So drop seeking and be a finder. You don't have to look very far; in fact, you don't have to look anywhere because this is it. You are the seer and knower of the manifestation. Without you, it cannot be.

Questioner: *The belief in a separate self drops away when awakening arises. On the other hand, we seem to cling most strongly to the fear of letting go and avoid going through psychological death. Would you talk about that?*

Tony: It doesn't have to happen. In a way, the mind still thinks, "Even Tony Parsons says the seeker has to drop away, and the cloud has to evaporate for the sun to be there." The mind immediately turns it into a process that has to take place. The mind always makes up a list of sequential steps that have to happen for awakening to take place. The mind sees awakening as a problem simply because it can't comprehend it. It does see, however, that when awakening happens, it will no longer sit on the throne. So don't hang on to the idea that steps have to take place, and if fear arises, accept it as part of the invitation. The story of awakening takes place in the mind, but the invitation to awaken happens in the body where you can feel fear, which manifests as "what is."

Questioner: *That's the genius of the ego doing its work.*

Tony: Yes, it's the "guru-mind," as I call it. The mind convinces you that it will take you to the goal. It's so brilliant that it will do everything in its power to convince you. It promises you that blessed event will happen "tomorrow," but it never does.

Questioner: *Would you talk about the invitation? What do you mean by "invitation"?*

Tony: For the mind that seeks to comprehend it, I would

explain it this way: Before this great adventure began—although it never really did begin and it will never end—we, who are pure Being, held a committee meeting and decided to play the game of manifestation, which, of course, includes the illusory idea of separation. We decided to split up into little bits and pretend to be separate beings who were no longer in touch with our own source. However, we also decided that at some point in the adventure we would want to come back home. We thought, "What's the best way of getting a passport back home?" We decided that everything that manifested would offer an invitation to return. This story means that everything you're looking at this moment is the source of all that is. Whether it's the wall, a piano, or a chair, everything comes from the source, the Absolute, which is unconditional love. Everyone is the One, playing the game of separation and pretending to be two.

Everything manifested comes from the source of light and love. Therefore, it is always at home in its original nature, which is what you are. You're looking at yourself manifesting as the flower or the wall. If you become intimate with any seemingly separate thing, you can lose your illusory separate self in that intimacy. It can die in that intimacy, just like making love. Sometimes, when we make love, we can vanish in the rapture of union. We can die to ourselves by being intimate with anything—the wall, the floor, another person, music, or feelings in the body. In each case, the beloved extends an invitation to the lover and says, "Come home." There isn't anything that isn't the beloved, and Being's sole purpose is to invite our apparently separate self to come home.

We live in total invitation. It excludes nothing, even emotional pain or anything that the mind thinks isn't spiritual or sacred. Everything is sacred because everything is the invitation. Nothing exists outside the invitation, which means that everything is the beloved. So you can never escape your own liberation. The seeker is always being invited, but when the seeker is no more, there's no need for the invitation, and everything becomes celebration.

Questioner: *Tony, do you have any idea why we decided to have this committee meeting?*
Tony: We didn't really; what I'm describing is only a parable. The whole of creation, this whole manifestation, appears to be a story, but it's actually only an invitation. We play the game of separation, knowing that at some point we'll come back home. The invitation to come home is built into everything, along with the forgetfulness that everything is really only a game. Some of us take the game so seriously that we believe that we're separate people, but a few of us remember who we really are. We agreed to these conditions before any of this actually began, including that we'd gather together to remind ourselves of the truth. So, hello again!

Questioner: *I understand this, but why did we choose this condition of separation?*
Tony: Essentially, unconditional love, which is potential energy, simply overflowed and manifested. The One manifested as the many through an explosion of energy. You are an overflowing of that love, and what you see around you is your own love overflowing into That. You *are* That. Let's be clear: Time, destiny, and choice don't exist at any level. There is only "this," which is a mystery that we can never fully understand.

Questioner: *Could you explain again how this apparent "self"*

INVITATION TO AWAKEN • 111

sees everything as the invitation?

Tony: You as an individual can't see everything as the invitation; only the wisdom within you knows this already. I'm speaking about a wisdom that's deeper than the individual. That wisdom sees the wonder of this constant, timeless invitation. The nearest that you can get to it (although there is no "you") is to apparently choose to be aware of it. Wherever your attention rests is the invitation. Like a butterfly in a garden that flits about, attention doesn't have to stay on one object, but can move from a feeling in the body to a car going by. In each case, wherever it rests is the beloved. If you bring your awareness to wherever it is right now, you'll meet the beloved. You're actually meeting yourself, so if you surrender or give yourself completely to whatever's happening, the illusory seeker may simply fade away, and you'll see the beloved, which is your original nature.

People have a misconception about formal meditation. Although there's nothing wrong with it, meditation may occur for some people and not for others. The difficulty with meditation is that a "me" is seeking a goal, which only reinforces the seeker. Whether we practice formal meditation or not, everybody is effortlessly living in the invitation at this moment.

Sometimes awakening happens to people who have no idea about anything we're talking about here. A book called *Super Consciousness Revisited* has accounts of ten such awakenings, six of them by people who have never heard of the words "enlightenment" or "meditation." As I see it, these awakenings happen simply because everyone is in the invitation.

Questioner: *Is every particle and object simultaneously in a* *state of apparent separation and reunion?*

Tony: No. Everything arises in That, and nothing can be except that which is. But in the game of separation, we believe in what we see, which is the external world. What the body/mind sees is a separate manifestation, an unreal world. When awakening arises and the sense of "me" drops away, what remains is the real world, which is simply a manifestation of unconditional love. One no longer sees separate people; one sees unconditional love "people-ing." That perception can take place only in consciousness, where the sense of "I am" arises as unconditional love, people-ing. The source of all this is pure Being.

Questioner: *So the objects of the world can be in apparent separation, yet they also can be in invitation simultaneously.*

Tony: That's always the case. The sense of separation and the disquiet that we feel about it *are* the invitation. In a way, you're being literal about it. You feel disquiet about your apparent separation from me, but it's an illusion. Just see that you are me and I am you. Of course, once you take up the invitation, it comes to an end. I don't live in invitation because there's no one here who needs it. In fact, no one here needs an invitation. In truth, you're inviting yourself to awaken to your own nature, to what you already are.

Questioner: *Does separation inherently have the invitation in it?*

Tony: Yes, that was your idea originally, and that's what all this is. The whole manifestation is totally meaningless, purposeless, without a story going on. What exists is simply the invitation.

Questioner: *You mentioned that some people simply became "awakened." Who decides which people are awakened and which aren't?*

Tony: No one does. There's no "will of God" and no such thing as "choice" anywhere. The idea of choice or will, which involves making up of the mind, is something that's created by the mind itself. Choice, which implies a motive, means that there's intentionality present, the idea that something is going somewhere, when in truth there isn't anything going anywhere. Choice and will are as illusory as karma and reincarnation, concepts made up by the mind.

Questioner: *One reason that there's no choice is that the apparent person is really a collection of thoughts, memories, and desires that inherently does not have a permanent life. Because of our conditioning, we think that we have choice, but we really don't, do we?*

Tony: In the end, there's no one. There never has been anyone, either. Therefore, "choice" can never exist because there's no one to do the choosing.

Questioner: *And this is really the appropriate understanding?*

Tony: Yes, except that it's beyond understanding. We can point out that there's no one here, but we can't "understand" it, since there's really no one there to understand it anymore. At one time I did understand this intellectually, but such understanding is generally meaningless.

Questioner: In an earlier meeting, I asked about the inability of the mind to grasp these very simple concepts. It really is obvious, upon reflection, that the mind can't really grasp them. I think that the advantage of a meeting such as this or an additional book . . .

Tony: What we're talking about goes beyond the words in a book. Have you ever read a book, and suddenly one sentence penetrated into you, almost bodily? I think these meetings are like that, and to some extent so are books, although not nearly as much. Meeting the "blood and bones" is where the most impact takes place. There's far more going on in this room than the words we're exchanging.

Questioner: Even though this is something that's not of the mind, it still takes some reminding.

Tony: It has to do with a resonance that's beyond intellectual understanding.

Questioner: Do you live continuously in a state of pure awareness?

Tony: First of all, there's no such thing as an awakened "person." People who appear to be awakened have nothing to do with it; they cannot in any way prolong or reduce it because there's no one who can choose either way. A person who claims to be enlightened cannot guarantee anything. Liberation involves accepting anything and everything. Nothing is denied, and if so-called "enlightened persons" are honest, they would explain that although there is only Be-ing, they sometimes contract into me-ing. But both are one in the liberated state. However, we've been conditioned to believe that enlightened beings live in a permanent state of bliss or pure Being.

Questioner: *You're not in continual surrender?*
Tony: There isn't anyone here to surrender. Be-ing is the case, but me-ing can also arise.

Questioner: *You seem to be continually aware that you're not there.*
Tony: I'm not continually aware that I'm not here because there's no one here. Within Being contraction can happen, but always within the perception of the whole. Anything can happen within the liberated state. Let's be very clear about this: I'm not an individual and not "someone" who has total wisdom and freedom and who can't possibly experience anger. Because I am "all that is," it can include anger, passion, or anything else that arises in consciousness. It can't be otherwise, since liberation is the total acceptance of all that is. If anger or lust arises in manifestation, it's all part of the divine expression. Whatever arises in the game is perfectly acceptable. We have the idea that once awakening happens, we arrive at a fixed state of blissful goodness. Nonsense! There's nothing good about me, which my wife Claire will confirm. Ask her and she'll tell you all the really awful things about me! Everything that arises as Tony Parsons, including all the knobby bits, all the funny bits, are part of the celebration, the richness, of the manifestation.

Questioner: *There's got to be something different between us; otherwise you wouldn't be there and I wouldn't be here.*

Tony: Let's catch it right there. Since there's no one "here," there's nothing to accept or reject. If you believe there's someone on the stage who's caught in a hypnotic dream, you're laboring under a misconception. Because there's no one here, there's nothing to accept or reject.

Questioner: *But there is somebody "here" who doesn't accept.*
Tony: That's what you believe. You have a powerful investment in that belief, which is just a wisp of smoke. So powerful is your belief that when you come to a meeting like this, you invest the speaker with a realization that you believe you don't have. Really, I'm the one who doesn't have anything. If there's a difference between us, it's that you have something and I have nothing. You're a rich man; you have "you" to cling to, while I'm at a disadvantage, being "no one" at all, except that I am good looking. [laughter]

Questioner: *You said that this apparent "non-person" can arise at any time. I assume that your identification with individuality is no longer possible. Once this transition happens, is it permanent?*
Tony: Yes, it is, but for no one. In this state of utter clarity, there isn't any belief, so I don't ask anything anymore. There's nothing to ask and no one to ask it.

Questioner: *How do you know that?*
Tony: I don't. I am That. I am the source of all that is, and so are you.

Questioner: *You mentioned that anything can happen, including expansion or contraction. Once that permanent shift* *happens and the sense of individuality drops away permanently, there's a continuum of awareness and constant awakeness that never goes away. The continuum exists whether the seeming world is there or not, whether your feelings contract or expand, or whether you feel depressed, angry, or happy. Underneath the waking or deep sleep states, there's a continuum of awareness and Being that's always lively and awake.*

Tony: Yes, that's so, that's how it is. Everyone here has feelings, thoughts, and sensations, but underneath them is utter stillness. This silence, this Being, is shouting louder than anything else in this room.

Questioner: *I'd like your perspective on two primary issues, which come up for me quite often: fear and external pressures. I mean this from the individual and societal viewpoints.*

Tony: Separation apparently happens when you're a very young child, and you suddenly no longer identify with the energy called "mother," but with a separate person called "Peter" or "Mary." That first moment of suddenly realizing that "I'm an individual, I'm on my own here," raises the most colossal fear. This fear comes from the sense of being in an alien world and feeling separate. For me, fear is the primary emotion that drives all the others. We all experience fear, and to comfort ourselves we build different "wombs" to protect and console ourselves from loss. But the strange joke is that even fear, which arises because of our sense of separation, is also the beloved, the invitation. It doesn't matter how safe the womb is. Even Bill Gates, with his billions of dollars of womb-life security, still lives in fear. Bill Gates is still damn scared.

Until separation evaporates, fear, which is really the beloved, will create nonsense dramas, such as "Am I going bankrupt?" or "Does she love me anymore?" If you truly look into fear, it has only one message: Come home. When you become intimate with fear—its texture, its rawness, the fire and flame of pain—just as in lovemaking, you can love the self. Then separation, which is the cause of that fear, just drops away. Fear can still arise again, but it can never live in the light of this awareness, which is the ground of everything.

What you call "external pressure" is simply another tool that creates fear. Actually, there isn't anything external because everything arises in consciousness. Although pressure in the form of your boss or traffic in Los Angeles appears to be "out there," it cannot be unless it arises in "I am." The boss can't arise except in awareness, nor can anything else. And everything that arises is absolutely, exquisitely, uniquely there as an invitation to awaken. Consider your friends, who seem to have slightly different problems from yours. You may actually see their problems far better than they can, and yet their apparent problems are uniquely theirs. They'll never work as an invitation for you. As part of the absolute genius of things, they will serve as an invitation uniquely set up for them.

Questioner: When you first began to experience your awakening, did the world become an unbearable place for you? In many ways, the world has become an unbearable place for me.

Tony: As I've said before, as long as there's a sense of separation, the world will be uncomfortable. Some people handle it better than others, but most find the world to be uncomfortable because of the sense of separation. In varying degrees, everything and everybody poses a threat to people. After the awakening of Tony Parsons, he discovered that he was in paradise. This is paradise. It wasn't that the world became bearable: it was seeing that "I am the world" and "The world is the beloved." At last, Tony Parsons was home because "I am That." It doesn't matter where you go, whether in New York, Cornwall, or Amsterdam: There is no difference because it's all home.

Questioner: *I live with a man who appears to be in "the desert." As he becomes increasingly sensitive, the world becomes more and more painful to him. Will this change?*
Tony: Oh, yes. I never went through the desert, nor do many other people have to. Not everybody has to go through the dark night of the soul. Joy can jump into greater joy, which is how it was for me. However, I know some people in London who are in the desert for whom the world has become more unbearable because their sensitivity has increased. As the sensitivity grows, life may become more painful or threatening. For other people, neurotic states can arise in the apparent body/mind that lead to greater conflict with their surroundings. The mind, which is filled with resistance, will fight with everything in its arsenal. These reactions may happen to some people and not to others.

Questioner: *Part of the pain that my wife spoke about comes from a stark, sharp-edged clarity, an awareness without the juice of love. Sometimes American technological, material society feels like a realm in hell.*

Tony: To people who are going through such experiences, I say, "What hasn't yet taken place in the desert is the 'falling in love.'" You have to come back to the intimacy with the beloved. If you ask for nothing but to meet the lover, you'll give up everything else. It's not enough to have a lukewarm attitude, such as, "Oh well, can I meet the lover?" You must feel, "I'm ready to give up everything to meet the lover." The Kingdom of Heaven is like a pearl in the field, and the farmer sells everything he has to obtain it. Intimacy with "this" is a mini-death, a readiness to die and open the floodgates to fall in love with the beloved.

Questioner: *Several years ago, I set about stilling the mind, using the force of my will. I wound up altering brain functioning, and I nearly became psychotic. I find the experience of a still mind to be quite awful and barren. I don't really want it, but it's useful because it gives some space from the mind's restlessness. Now the stillness comes and goes while thoughts come up within it, but there's a problem in that the stillness feels dissociated from love. In a way, it's probably a defense.*

Tony: Yes, but it's not a permanent casualty.

Questioner: *No?*

Tony: Although it's fairly uncommon, dissociation can happen in someone who has a very powerful determination. One appears to have stilled the mind, but in dissociation one actually moves into something quite barren and split from life. As far as I'm concerned, the idea of the mind being stilled is a contradiction in terms. I wonder whether something else was actually happening to you. The mind can only be the mind; there can't be a "still" mind. I don't need to still my mind because I am stillness itself. The mind with its constant activity exists within that stillness. Most people have a misconception about stilling the mind. I *am* the stillness, and the mind arises within it.

Questioner: *Do you think that my approach was too detached and mental?*

Tony: The more masculine approach (which has nothing to do with men) leans towards the mental and values stillness, while the feminine approach emphasizes intimacy and aliveness. Our conditioning in both Eastern and Western traditions favors the male approach to divinity. This is like the joke I told yesterday about the monk who was translating the scriptures and discovered the word wasn't "celibate," but rather "celebrate." Becoming a monk is attractive, especially for men. In our time, a marriage is taking place between the East and the West, and the results are a bit frightening as the creativity of the West meets the perfectionist attitude of the East. One approach is very juicy and alive, while the other one is very dry. If this meeting takes place in That, then intimacy with the beloved will naturally arise.

Questioner: *What exactly are the different attitudes between the East and West?*

Tony: My sense is that the Eastern approach involves the perfection of the ascetic, whereas the Western approach, which is primarily Christian, emphasizes marriage, the joining of creative, alive energies in an impersonal manner. These two approaches are now coming together in great clarity, which is what awakening is: the marriage of the apparent individual with the whole. Your approach has been primarily ascetic. Now you need to open your heart to the lover.

Questioner: *My friend refuses to vote. What is the value of being socially active since, as you say, that nothing is really happening anyway?*

Tony: There's no one who can do anything or who has any sense of how things should be. There's no compromise about this. All I'm saying is that our apparent world is only an appearance. It's happening within us, and what we see in the outer world is an expression of what arises in awareness. At this point in the drama, I see a marriage taking place between East and West, between male and female, both religiously and politically. The male approach has had its time, and now the two are marrying at all sorts of levels.

What I'm saying to you is that there's nobody in this world, so there's nobody who can *do* anything about what's happening. Things either will happen or they won't. There are no "shoulds," because no separate person exists who should or could change anything.

Questioner: *When questioning the meaning of life, Joseph Campbell said, "You give meaning to your own life."*
Tony: How can you give meaning to your own life when you don't have a life?

Questioner: *I see that you've got a wedding ring. Evidently, you fell in love and got married.*
Tony: Falling in love happened. Fortunately, I married someone who wasn't there either, although she still insists on combing my hair after I've already done it!

Questioner: *In this moment, I see clearly that there's nobody here. I realize that who I am is not an object or a thing, but a no-thing. This realization happened in spite of me; I had nothing to do with it. Through exposure to Tony Parsons and others, this "seeing" just happens.*

Whatever I've consciously done to awaken has always taken me further away from it. Sometimes greater awakeness arises by itself. Now, for example, there's nobody here. When this awakening happens, are we established in nothing?
Tony: Yes, absolutely. There's a moment when your perception suddenly changes, but before and after this shift, you're established in Being. In effect, the "me" that's falling away *seems* to become more profound. It isn't in reality because it's profound by nature, yet it appears like that to one who becomes aware of it.

Questioner: *It was a pleasure listening to you on Friday and Saturday, and today it seems even deeper.*
Tony: Since there's nothing here when "That" sees its own source, it sees its own nothingness. In other words, you're the one talking to yourself.

Questioner: *You've said that everything comes from consciousness, including our story line, which is completely purposeless. How does our story line come about? Is it all mind-stuff that we need to drop, or is there some meaning behind the story of our life and the choices we've made?*
Tony: It's all a dream. Consciousness uses the mind to create a linear story, which takes the apparent person on a journey toward somewhere. The whole thing is a total illusion. We're so convinced that we've lived for thirty years, that certain events have happened at certain places, and that we're individuals living in a life story. All of it is meaningless except the invitation we have every moment to see that we're the source.

Questioner: *So we really have no choices at all?*
Tony: There isn't anyone to have them.

Questioner: *Then the apparent self has no choice at all?*
Tony: No. There is no apparent self. It's an illusory arising, which can't do anything about its own dissolution. The illusory self can't make itself vanish because it's already illusory.

Questioner: *Within that level of the illusion, do we have choice?*
Tony: No. There's no one there, and there's no such thing as choice. There isn't even anything that chooses. There's no such thing as choice or will at all. Not only is there no individual with a choice but there's no such thing as choice.

Questioner: *Even though it seems to me . . .*
Tony: It only appears that way.

Questioner: *But I made the choice to be here today, didn't I?*
Tony: No. Nobody did.

Questioner: *I could have chosen not to come and almost did, but I didn't. I really didn't have a choice about that, either?*
Tony: Not at all. Somebody in Wales woke up one Saturday morning, knowing that she wasn't going to see Tony Parsons. She walked out of her house and went down the road with the idea of what she was going to do, but it definitely didn't include seeing Tony Parsons. She got on the train, went to London, and arrived at our meeting, even though she apparently had no intention of seeing Tony Parsons that day.

Questioner: *Does the mind become irrelevant when it sees this illusion for what is it?*
Tony: The mind doesn't accept is own irrelevancy. But when the mind gives up and becomes inactive, your original nature simply arises.

Questioner: Can the mind get to a point that it realizes it has nothing to do with an apparent me?

Tony: The mind is only a tool of the source, which creates consciousness and uses the mind to create form. The mind can't do anything about being a tool. It can't decide anything because there's nothing to decide; it's just a tool to create the thought forms of manifestation.

Questioner: When there is awakening, it seems that the mind becomes more intelligent.

Tony: The mind is very useful. It's brilliant at playing with computers and coming up with "enlightened" ideas, but there's no role that the mind plays in furthering awakening. When the mind no longer functions as the primary energy, we awaken to our fundamental nature. As a tool, the mind can't reach awakening. The mind can give you great understanding about what enlightenment isn't, but it only brings you to the river's edge.

Questioner: After awakening, which has nothing to do with the mind, does the light of this awakening keep the mind from creating the "me"-sense on an ongoing basis?

Tony: Absolutely.

Questioner: It's really the light of awareness that makes the mind more intelligent, not the mind itself.

Tony: Yes, absolutely. After awakening, we use the mind as a tool and nothing more.

Questioner: So it's really acting efficiently in doing its job and not creating nonsense.

Tony: Let's be clear about this: The mind is actually just a collection of thoughts. There's no independent entity called "mind." This collection of thoughts invariably spins threads, such as "I don't get this," "Life is threatening," "Have I paid my phone bill?" and "I'd like to be with a blonde at the beach." After awakening, the blonde still comes up, but it's a better quality blonde!

Questioner: *You said that at some point a definite shift in perception occurs. What is that event? What happens in that shift?*
Tony: Let's call it an event. It involves dropping the "me."

Questioner: *Even though the "me" dwindles to almost nothing, is there a point at which it's entirely dropped?*
Tony: Yes. It definitely drops when we have the sudden perception "I am That." Thereafter, we can still move back into the sense of "me," but we do it within an underlying ground of awareness, which witnesses our contraction back into the previous identification. So the play between me-ing and be-ing goes on, except that be-ing moves from the body to the forefront of our life. Being watches both the identification and non-identification with the "me."

I really can't explain how Tony Parsons vanished halfway across the park. I'm getting into an area I can't describe. All that was there, which is always there, is "I am That." It's not that I'm one with the trees and I know what it's like to be bark, an idea I find quite ridiculous. I've really tried to find words that could describe this, but I really can't.

Questioner: *How does what you're describing relate to the sense of falling in love that you spoke about earlier?*

Tony: It's utterly beyond that. Is there anybody here who can help? [laughter].

Questioner: *Transformation always seems radical, like jumping off a cliff into an abyss. In stories I've heard, that's how noticeable shifts in consciousness take place.*

Tony: It doesn't always have to be so dramatic. Someone I know in London named Roger, who was coming to my talks, was so open to the understanding that "there's no one" that he didn't need to ask any questions about it. He came to one of our retreats in which the final awakening happened, but it wasn't a big event, a big "WOW," but rather an ordinary "wow." Before the retreat he told me that Roger was still hanging around but had become quite transparent. Then on that morning, the final shift occurred suddenly and undramatically. That's the nearest I can express it.

Questioner: *During this lovely weekend, the "me," which normally spends so much time seeking, hasn't had much room to express itself, so it's been dissolving. However, while it's dissolving, it's exhausting to watch it clutch at its pent-up fears.*

Tony: The "me" is exhausted anyway, having spent twenty or thirty years continuously constructing itself. Every morning it constructs "me" and then has to keep "me" together. It really wears you out. Many people experience a tremendous relief when they understand that all this effort to sustain the self is unnecessary.

Questioner: I'm feeling exhausted, maybe from a fear of being released. As the fear dissolves, it wants to protect itself by re-establishing itself but can't. Can you speak a little bit more on this?

Tony: The beloved invites you through all the senses, including cognizance. The purpose of the senses is to return home through them. We contact the beloved through sensory aliveness—through what we hear, taste, touch, smell, and cognize. When thoughts arise, they are the beloved thinking. There's nothing wrong with thoughts, which are witnessed as they arise and pass away. There's no escape from that which always is. The beloved invites you through the senses, cognizance, and intimacy with whatever is to lose the illusory self.

Questioner: Religious traditions talk about the illusory self getting stronger through the fulfillment of the senses.

Tony: Religious or traditional ideas about awareness and awakening often come from deep ignorance. The beloved has no interest in scriptures or traditions, which are within the realm of the mind. The beloved is alive in the immediate, timeless wonder of presence. The mind has a hard time with this immediacy since it brings about the death of the mind and the self. The mind, which fears its own dissolution, wants excitement and great drama. We have religious theology and scriptures because they offer great dramas and theories about God. What's frightening to the mind about presence is that it's ordinary and not very dramatic. [picks up an object] The weight of this object, which isn't very dramatic, is the beloved.

Questioner: *In the "desert" that you spoke of earlier, your senses are highly aware. How do we experience the beloved through the senses when we're in the desert, especially since it's so unbearable and overwhelming?*

Tony: Let's be clear about this: One never experiences the beloved. There's only the beloved, and even when the happening is over, there's still the beloved. The whole idea of experiencing the beloved is illusory. If, as you say, being in the desert somehow exaggerates and stimulates the sense of "what is," that's just a stronger invitation from the beloved. It offers a stronger possibility to die into "what is." You should forget about the idea of being in the desert because the mind will go on thinking, "I'm still in the desert and still have forty miles to go." Drop the desert entirely, and simply be in "this," allowing it to be.

Conclusion

We've been communicating all day. Shall we be quiet for a while? Close your eyes or keep them open since whatever arises is the beloved. Let there be no one and nothing, but whatever arises.

These dialogues often include concepts that address the mind's complexity, but in the end they point only to the utter simplicity and wonder of what is.

As you read these words, there is a *knowing* which embraces this activity. It is a recognition of that which has always been. When you took your first breath and saw your first day; when you eat, sleep, run or walk, drink tea or peel potatoes: There it is—that which knows and is aware. Through all the struggles, the apparent failures and successes, within all the adventures that seem to be the story of your life, there is the one constant that never comes and never goes away—it is presence.

This book speaks only of that and reminds us of a fragrance, the stillness and silence that is home. This is all there is.

About the Author

TONY PARSONS was born in London in 1933. At the age of twenty, he spontaneously awoke to the rediscovery of his true nature. Throughout the years, he shared this "open secret" with like-minded friends. Only since 1996, when Tony began to communicate the nature of his experience through writings, did people from all over the world begin to deeply resonate with the message he shares.

Tony brings a deep maturity and a lifetime of spiritual understanding to his talks and published works. The clarity and completely natural manner in which he writes and speaks about living in the unlimited awareness of Presence is refreshingly authentic.

Meetings and residentials with Tony Parsons take place regularly in the U. K. and internationally.

For details, visit the website at: www.theopensecret.com

Alternatively, you can write to Tony Parsons at:
The Open Secret
c/o HDTV and Media
Cranborne, Dorset BH21 5PZ
UNITED KINGDOM

About Inner Directions

InnerDirections Publishing is the imprint of the Inner Directions Foundation, a nonprofit organization dedicated to exploring self-discovery and awakening to one's essential nature.

We publish distinctive book and video titles that express the heart of authentic spirituality. Each of our titles presents an original perspective, with a clarity and insight that can only come from the experience of ultimate reality. These unique publications communicate the immediacy of *That* which is eternal and infinite within us: the nondualistic ground from which religions and spiritual traditions arise.

Inner Directions depends upon the support of people like you—friends who recognize the merit of an organization whose sole purpose is to disseminate works of enduring spiritual value. To receive our catalog or to find out how you can help sponsor an upcoming publishing project, call, write, or e-mail:

Inner Directions
P. O. Box 130070
Carlsbad, CA 92013

Tel: 760 599-4075
Fax: 760 599-4076
Orders: 800 545-9118

E-mail: mail@InnerDirections.org
Website: www.InnerDirections.org